YORK N

General Editors: P
of Stirling) & Prof
University of Beiri

Dylan Thomas

UNDER MILK WOOD

Notes by Colin Meir
MA (DUBLIN) PH D (ESSEX)
Reader in English Literature, Ulster Polytechnic

LONGMAN
YORK PRESS

All extracts from *Under Milk Wood* by Dylan Thomas, published by J. M. Dent & Sons Ltd, are reprinted by kind permission.

YORK PRESS
Immeuble Esseily, Place Riad Solh, Beirut.

LONGMAN GROUP LIMITED
Burnt Mill,
Harlow, Essex

First published 1983
ISBN 0 582 78207 4
Printed in Hong Kong by
Wilture Enterprises (International) Ltd.

Contents

Part 1

Introduction

The life of Dylan Thomas

Dylan Marlais Thomas was born on 27 October 1914, in Swansea, South Wales.* When he died in New York on 9 November 1953, at the age of thirty-nine, he had already become something of a legend in his own time. In contrast to the prevailing mood of the poetry immediately before the Second World War, which was introspectively concerned with matters of social and political conscience, the work of Dylan Thomas, intensely evocative in both sound and imagery, was in joyous celebration of life; his poems were written, as his own note to his collected volume affirms, 'for the love of Man and in praise of God'. But it was at least as much in response to the poet himself as to the kind of poetry he produced that Thomas's popular reputation grew. For an audience recently released from wartime discipline and austerity, he came to represent a romantic idealisation of the improvident and alcoholic bohemian who is gifted with magic speech, a view which Thomas both fostered and satirised. No other modern poet has excited such interest; but the fact that his *Collected Poems*, published in November 1952, sold 10,000 copies within the first year is not solely due to the appeal of the poetry and to the attractiveness of the image of irresponsible genius. Dylan Thomas was the first poet of stature to use the newly expanding mass media of communication as a vehicle for his work. More than a decade before the success of the 'pop poets' of the 1960s, through broadcasts, recordings, and public readings he gained a wide audience for a poetry which in subject and language is much more complex than theirs. That he is the only poet popularly referred to simply by his first name marks an intimacy of public attention and acclaim approaching that normally reserved for stars of the stage or screen. But this unprecedented relationship between poet and audience depended to a great extent upon the way the former presented his material; it placed a theatrical emphasis on personality and performance which made it difficult to see behind the figure of the heavy-drinking, gregarious entertainer that of the painstaking artist; and although Dylan Thomas never completely sacrificed the one to the other, it was

*This summary relies for most of its facts, though not for its opinions, on the most recent biography of the poet: Paul Ferris, *Dylan Thomas*, Hodder & Stoughton, London, 1977; this is also available in an edition published by Penguin Books, Harmondsworth.

his playing up to the public image of himself that helped to bring about his early death at the end of two exhausting lecture tours of the United States undertaken within the same year. While the common report that the poet had died of drink was a too readily accepted simplification of the facts, it was nonetheless clearly established that alcoholism was a major contributory cause.

The drinking was linked to another aspect of the poet as performer which contained a bitter contradiction. Many of Thomas's admirers would have found it impossible to reconcile what they saw as inspired rhetoric with a creative process which called for the use of a word-finding dictionary. Like most artists, Thomas had to work very hard in order to give the impression that what he wrote flowed naturally from his pen; in his case, however, that necessary artifice disguised something else which had nothing whatsoever to do with art: the sense of spontaneous linguistic power that the poetry evoked for the listener ironically masked the poet's own desperate fear of not being able to write at all. Despite the imaginative energy of his verse and the confident sonority of his voice in reading it, Dylan Thomas was unsure of himself; and after his first successes in London in the mid 1930s, he became increasingly unsure of his creative abilities. His reputation rests on a relatively small output, which decreased almost in inverse proportion to the growth of his following. Nearly half of the eighty-nine poems in the 1952 collected volume had been written by 1936; and in the last four and a half years of his life he completed only six poems. From 1950 onwards, just at the point when his earnings were being fairly substantially boosted by the four lucrative trips he made to America, Thomas claimed with frantic insistence that money worries were depriving him of the peace needed for his writing. While there is no doubt that such worries were often merely an excuse for not writing, it is clear that the poet found it necessary to convince himself otherwise. By categorically stating that there is no evidence to suggest that Thomas was hounded to death by financial distress, Paul Ferris's uncompromising biography exposes yet another romantic fallacy about the poet. The real cause of his insecurity lay elsewhere. In addition to factors concerning the nature of Thomas's talent and the demands made on him by his post-war audience, it has to do with matters of upbringing and personality which can only be briefly outlined here.

The single most enduring influence on Dylan Thomas was that of his father, D. J. Thomas, who had nurtured his son's first responses to literature and was in part responsible for his ambition to be a poet. D. J. Thomas was a successful Senior English teacher at Swansea Grammar School, but he felt he deserved a better academic position, and he aspired to a higher social position than he could afford. His conscious sense of superiority as a man of letters did not falsify his deep love of his subject, but he felt that circumstances had frustrated his own creative potential as a writer. Although both he and his wife were bilingual, he banned the speaking of Welsh in the family because he believed that in order to get on in the world Welshmen had to speak English; yet he gave his son first names which identify him with Welsh native tradition: 'Dylan' (the word means 'sea' or 'ocean') is a rather obscure figure from the Welsh medieval epic, *Mabinogion*; 'Marlais' is taken from the bardic name chosen by the poet's great uncle, who was an Eisteddfod bard* of some repute. This evocation of Welsh inheritance through names marks D. J. Thomas's emotional affinities; nonetheless, the social claims predominated so strongly that not only did he refuse to teach his son Welsh, but he also went to the extreme of giving him elocution lessons so that he would not speak English with a Welsh accent. Even in the somewhat pretentiously Anglicised suburb of the Uplands in Swansea, where the Thomases lived, the absence of local pronunciation or accent in Dylan's voice was so extraordinary that his friends nicknamed him 'Lord Cut-Glass'. D. J. Thomas's elocution lessons were accompanied by frequent readings from English literature, particularly from Shakespeare, whose poetry was apparently being quoted to the boy even before he could talk. Nothing is known of the methods used in this remarkable feat of 'educating' the boy's voice to avoid normal environmental influences, but what is amply documented by the many public readings that Dylan Thomas gave and by the recordings he made is the exceptional importance to the poet of the sound of words, a fact which is further supported by the consensus of critical opinion about his work. The composer, Daniel Jones (*b.* 1912), the poet's boyhood friend, speaks of the richness of his voice, and of the mesmeric effect of his incantatory reading style, which proceeds at so measured a pace that the count of the syllables can be clearly heard. Indeed his verse structure sometimes relies more on syllabic patterning than on metric stress, which identifies it with Welsh rather than English poetic practice. Unforeseen as this ironic outcome of D. J. Thomas's voice-tutoring certainly must have been, it is clear that in his father's eyes Dylan was destined to succeed in both spheres where his own achievement had fallen far short of his wishes, both socially and professionally as a poet. But his influence was felt at a deeper level than those aims. A moving testimony of the poet's love is given in 'Do not go gentle into that good night', where he urges his terminally sick father to face death with righteous anger against its inevitability:

> And you, my father, there on the sad height,
> Curse, bless, me now with your fierce tears, I pray.
> Do not go gentle into that good night.
> Rage, rage against the dying of the light.

*The Eisteddfod is the annual Welsh festival of poetry and music.

With a telling simplicity, the last line of the unfinished 'Elegy' on his father's death states: 'Until I die he will not leave my side.'

Dylan Thomas himself speaks of two other main sources for his love of language: nursery rhymes and the Bible. An example of the long-term effect of the former source has been given recently by a critic who points out that Thomas incorporates almost unchanged a line from a Victorian nursery rhyme into one of his late poems; and we may notice with what felicity children's songs and rhyming games are brought into *Under Milk Wood.* The influence of the Bible again lay – initially at least – with the poet's father, who, although agnostic, frequently quoted from it. There are records of the boy's attendance, before he was five years old, at the Walter Road Congregational Church near the Uplands; and even though his parents were not chapel-goers, Dylan could not have escaped the influence of the Welsh non-conformist tradition of eloquent preaching. His own uncle, David Rees, is reported as having the gift, not uncommon among popular Welsh preachers, of being able to work his sermon into a religious fervour of words, called a 'hwyl'. Certainly, both Thomas's method of reading his poetry and his use of particular syntactical patterns in his verse and in his serious prose suggest biblical influences on his work.

A third factor determining the nature of the poet's upbringing concerns his being excessively indulged by his parents and others. He was a beautiful child, but his mother insisted he was of delicate health; she said he had frequent attacks of asthma and suffered from acute anaemia. However hypochondriac her attitude may have been – and there are reports of the boy running in cross-country races, which would seem to argue against Mrs Thomas's view of her son's physical condition – he did manage to spend a lot of time in bed, where he was able to satisfy his voracious appetite for reading. When, at the age of eleven, he moved from the shabby-genteel private Dame School* he had attended for three years, up to the Grammar School, he was further protected by the fact that his father taught there. The boy was apparently able to get away with truancy or with half-baked excuses for misdemeanours, and to stay on at school when his academic results in most subjects other than English, in which he excelled, were appalling. His exploitation of this situation added an indulgent element to that preoccupation with the self which is naturally fostered by the inward gaze of the budding poet. On the personal and moral level it impeded his growth to maturity and probably contributed to his sense of insecurity as an adult, as well as to the facility with which he later fulfilled the self-regarding roles expected of him. On the artistic level, the fact that such a large proportion of his work is about that lost world of childhood and adolescence points to a serious limitation of his imaginative range.

*A fee-paying school for children with a woman teacher or head teacher.

A final consideration has to do with setting. As a seaport town, Swansea was divided between rural and urban influences, just as it was between the Welsh working class and those people who, like Thomas's parents, aspired to a higher social position. Nonetheless, the poet's roots on both sides of the family were in rural Wales. At more than one level there was from the beginning a dislocation between the sources of the poet's imaginative energy and the avenues in which it could find recognition. Brief as his periods of creative activity were in the last years, they were concentrated in the remote villages of New Quay and Laugharne, where Dylan Thomas was at a blessed remove from the demands of his audience, if not from those of his family and his poetic conscience.

If there was any sense of insecurity at the beginning of Dylan Thomas's career, it did not affect the amount of work he produced. He published his first poem in the School Magazine when he was just eleven years old; and although it was a year before his second piece of light verse appeared there, that was soon to be followed by much more frequent contributions up to 1931. The first poem for which he was actually paid was, however, not his own at all. On 14 January 1927, the *Western Mail* printed a poem called 'His Requiem', signed D. M. Thomas; and it was not until 1971 that its true source came to light: the poem had first appeared in the *Boy's Own Paper* for November 1923, above the name of Lillian Gard. As with Thomas's foiled attempt at plagiarism concerning a poem sent to the School Magazine two years later in 1929, this incident is perhaps best viewed in terms of a schoolboy prank. But it does also point to a need to advertise himself as a poet, which has some bearing upon his later behaviour.

On the other hand, to be irreverent about authorship, as about many other matters, was part of the pose he was trying to adopt; for example, he mocked the accepted view of poetic composition by collaborating with Daniel Jones on the mechanical basis of alternate authorship, Jones supplying the odd-numbered and Thomas the even-numbered lines. Some two hundred poems came out of this process; and Jones asserts that while a few of these were printed in the School Magazine under Thomas's initials, many others appeared there which were Thomas's but were never identified as his. Whatever games were played with sacrosanct literary attitudes, the work Thomas collected in his four 'Note Books', which he kept between 1930 and 1934, shows that the notion of being a poet was no longer merely a pose: his artistic commitment is defined in the quality and the subject-matter of the poetry. This was to be the most fertile period of Thomas's creative life. According to Daniel Jones, four-fifths of all the poetry Thomas ever produced was written at this time; what he called 'Mainly free verse poems' in the notebooks were to provide material for publication for many years to come, either as unchanged or, more frequently, as reworked sources; or as a combination of both.

Dylan Thomas left school at sixteen, having failed the Central Welsh Board School Certificate, and worked first as a proof-reader, then as an apprentice reporter for the *South Wales Daily Post*. For two to three years from 1932 he appeared regularly in the amateur productions of the Little Theatre in Swansea, where he enjoyed playing exuberant character parts. His circle of friends widened, he became more flamboyant in dress and manner, and began to drink fairly heavily. 'Old Garbo', one of the autobiographical stories in his *Portrait of the Artist as a Young Dog* (1940), tells of Thomas the Reporter on a pub-crawl in Swansea; other stories in the collection, such as 'One Warm Saturday', sensitively evoke adolescent sexuality. But while in real life Thomas liked to sport his sexual promiscuity as yet another badge of the bohemian poet, there was evidently more acting than action in this sphere, particularly when he was still in his teens. His drinking, on the other hand, may have begun as a game or as a gesture of rebellion against provincialism or as a way of proving himself a man of the world, but it soon passed from being merely a performance to being a trademark which later in his life became almost a necessity. By the end of 1932 he had lost his job through irresponsible reporting, and was obliged to operate as a freelance. Apart from a brief period during the 1940s, this was to be his position for the rest of his life. To be freelance fitted the identity of the nonconformist writer, but in Thomas's case it cost dear, for the inevitable financial uncertainty was subsequently to contribute to the pressures which he felt were preventing him from producing new work.

His first poem published in the English press, 'And death shall have no dominion', appeared in the *New English Weekly* for 17 May 1933; and soon afterwards another poem, which has not survived, was read on the BBC.* In August of the same year he went to London, probably for the first time, where he met at least two influential editors. He began to send poems to various papers and periodicals, including the *Sunday Referee*, through whose pages he met Pamela Hansford Johnson, herself a contributor to the paper's 'Poetry Corner'. Their relationship, which later developed into a love affair, took its start from an exchange of letters; and his to her (nearly half of which were written before they actually met in February 1934), provide a revealing picture of the poet's personality and of his attitude to his art. He is comically self-deprecating about his small stature, and makes jokes about the state of his health; in both cases, the light-hearted humour conceals preoccupations that were real enough to stay with him for the rest of his life. About poetry,

*The British Broadcasting Corporation, the non-commercial radio and television network in Britain.

however, these letters are intensely serious and explicit: they define Thomas's critical viewpoints on other people's poetry, including Miss Johnson's, and disclose some of his own principles of composition. In an undated letter (probably of early October 1933) he advises Miss Johnson first to select imagery to suit mood then thought to fit image, which is exactly the process he outlines five years later when describing his own methods to Henry Treece (1912–66), the author of the first book-length study of his work. In November 1933, he writes that 'the description of a thought or action – however abstruse it may be – can be beaten home by bringing it onto a physical level. Every idea, intuitive or intellectual, can be imagined and translated in terms of the body, its flesh, skin, blood, sinews, veins, glands, organs, cells, or senses.'

It is the physical basis of the imagery in the poetry of Thomas's first collection, *18 Poems*, which distinguishes it from his earlier work. The volume came out in December 1934, its contents being chosen exclusively from poetry written since August 1933. Thomas's next collection, *Twenty-five Poems*, which in 1936 began his lifelong association with the publishing house of J. M. Dent & Sons, was drawn largely from work completed earlier than the poems of the previous volume. Ignorance of this fact caused critical puzzlement for years after the poet's death, since the second publication unaccountably seemed less sure of its direction in form and content than the first. Both volumes were on the whole very well received at the time, but it was Edith Sitwell's (1887–1964) enthusiastic review of *Twenty-five Poems* in the *Sunday Times* which brought Thomas a wider audience and began his climb to fame.

In November 1934 he had gone to live in a bed-sitter* in London, in what he called 'the quarter of the pseudo-artists', where it appears he was determined to play the part of the dissolute poet. He met a number of the literary and artistic figures of the day, including the historian A. J. P. Taylor (*b.*1906) and his wife Margaret, who became his most generous benefactor, and two well-known critics, Geoffrey Grigson (*b.*1905) and Cyril Connolly (1903–74). It was Augustus John (1878–1961), the celebrated bohemian portrait painter, who introduced Thomas sometime early in 1936 to Caitlin Macnamara (*b.*1913), a former dancer who was one of John's models. Caitlin later explained that her sexual relationship with the painter, like that of all his other models, was merely a matter of enhancing his reputation as a Casanova; nonetheless, her attachment to Thomas caused jealousies between the two men. Caitlin and Dylan married in July 1937, and after staying in Cornwall and Kent moved to a primitive cottage in Laugharne, their first home together. It was a tempestuous marriage: there were quick quarrels and equally rapid reconciliations; Caitlin, fiery and headstrong,

*A rented furnished room, serving as both bedroom and living-room.

cared little for social proprieties, but she provided a secure enough domestic background to enable the poet to work steadily for the first time since he left his home in Swansea. His friend Vernon Watkins (1906–67) later said that this period at the house called 'Sea View', to which they soon moved from the cottage, was the happiest of Thomas's life. By the end of 1938 he was back in 'nightmare London' again, where he met the novelists Lawrence Durrell (*b.*1912) and Henry Miller (1891–1981). Caitlin gave birth to a boy, Llewelyn, on 30 January 1939.

During 1938 and 1939 Thomas wrote the autobiographical stories contained in *Portrait of the Artist as a Young Dog* (1940), whose title was picked up from James Joyce's (1882–1941) famous novel, *A Portrait of the Artist as a Young Man* (1916). Characteristically, Thomas changed the last word of his title into an ironic reference to the adolescent who tries to be a man about town; or, if the last word is read backwards, whose god-like youth is marked by kinds of embarrassment and failure which have more in common with the stories of *Dubliners* (1914) than with Joyce's first novel. The stories in *The Map of Love* (1939), a volume which also contained poems, were completed between 1934 and 1937. Parts of some of Thomas's stories written during this period were considered too obscene to print; others were surrealistic in mode; and certainly few of those selected for the 1939 publication could be seen as straightforward narrative. The stories of *Portrait of the Artist as a Young Dog*, on the other hand, being very readily accessible to most readers, represent a movement from obscurity to clarity in Thomas's prose which is continued in his film scripts and radio talks of the 1940s, and which culminates in *Under Milk Wood.* His poetry is never at any time as simple and direct as the prose written from 1938 onwards; and it is not until the mid 1940s that a less complex and involved style appears, as in 'Poem in October' and 'Fern Hill', which rapidly became favourite anthology choices partly because there is nothing in form or image to obstruct the reader's or the listener's understanding.

Neither *The Map of Love* nor *Portrait of the Artist as a Young Dog* did very well, their sales being affected by the outbreak of war in 1939. The Thomases had been living a hand-to-mouth existence ever since their marriage, and debts were accumulating. Money had been advanced by Dent under various contracts which the poet had failed to fulfil, and he tried to appease his publisher by writing a novel, *Adventures in the Skin Trade*, which was never completed, about a young man who comes up to London from Wales. Thomas's notions of becoming a conscientious objector or of obtaining a reserved occupation came to nothing, but he was able to avoid conscription by failing the medical examination. During the summer of 1940 he and Caitlin went to live with the wealthy John Davenport, with whom he wrote a novel called *The Death of the King's Canary* (not published until 1976), which satirises contemporary writers and artists. While at the Davenports' until the autumn of that year, Thomas also wrote a couple of short scripts for the BBC, and was later commissioned to do further script work for broadcasting and for films. Late in 1941 he obtained a regular job at Strand Films, where for the next three years he helped produce scripts for ten or more documentaries. The task of supplying words for what is seen on the screen had a direct influence on the style of *Under Milk Wood*, where voices have to incorporate the function of the camera at strategically introductory sections of the radio play.

The war years were spent in London and in Wales. There are tales, almost certainly exaggerated, of Thomas's infidelities with other women when he was left alone in London. His circle of friends naturally widened through his work in films and at the BBC, and it was during these years that the poet's public personality took its definite shape. For all his kindness and warmth as a private individual, he seemed to be being driven to constant performance as an entertainer, drinker, raconteur, and anarchic destroyer of accepted norms of social behaviour. The reasons are too complex for easy solution, and Paul Ferris, his biographer, is clearly aware that it is only part of the issue to state, recording John Davenport's view, that 'the ultimate tragedy of Thomas was that he lost his lyrical gift and was left with nothing but a public personality, which he despised.' It may well be that the poet shared his wife's scorn for the kind of writing he was employed to do during this time; at all events, it was his return to Wales in July 1944, to a cottage at Blaen Cwm, which signalled a new burst of creative energy, issuing in some eight poems within a twelvemonth period, including 'Fern Hill' which was published in *Deaths and Entrances* (1946), a volume which re-established his poetic reputation. Later in the summer of 1944 the family (which now included a daughter, Aeron, born in March 1943) moved to New Quay, Cardiganshire, the village which provides the background for the radio talk 'Quite Early One Morning', produced for the Welsh network of the BBC at the end of 1944. This talk and the radio feature which he wrote in 1947 called 'Return Journey' mark stages of development towards *Under Milk Wood.*

After another brief stay in London, in other people's homes, through the autumn and winter of 1945–6, the Thomases lived in or near Oxford until 1949 in accommodation provided by Mrs Margaret Taylor, the historian's wife. The poet's work in London during this time, on film scripts and on radio, earned him a very good income, but he still managed to be short of money. The family moved back to Wales in the spring of 1949, to the Boat House at Laugharne which Margaret Taylor had bought; by the end of that year, in which their third child, Colm, was born, a backlog of income tax debts put the poet's financial position into permanent jeopardy and made the long looked-for trip to America the following year a necessity. He had not been writing much poetry and had also failed to fulfil various contracts with the BBC, for at least one of which he had been partly paid in advance. He gave extremely successful readings of his own and of other poets' work on the American university circuit* from late February to early June 1950; and the sense of freedom from problems which he could not solve at home, combined with a self-conscious irreverence towards academic and social proprieties, produced an intensification of his by now familiar role of drunken exhibitionism about which tales have grown legion and legendary across America. As always, his promiscuity was more suggestion than fact; but the change from beer to spirits must have accelerated the damage heavy drinking was doing to his health throughout this tour and the three other tours he was to make in America.

From this point on the die is cast, it seems almost wilfully, for the end. Thomas earned two thousand eight hundred pounds on his first tour, which was a princely sum for a writer at the time, but he was soon asking Margaret Taylor for money; and when tax was later imposed on these earnings he was thrown even further into debt. During the next eighteen months Thomas's occasional freelance radio and script work did little to help his finances, and he was forced to make appeals to various benefactors, couched in self-deprecating, tragi-comic terms. The begging letters got written while several literary projects remained unfinished, including *Under Milk Wood*, for part of which he had already received an advance of a hundred pounds from the Italian magazine *Botteghe Oscure*. It was the same story when Thomas and his wife, who had gone with him this time, returned from the second American tour, which lasted from 20 January to 16 May 1952. He again took up freelance radio and script-writing work, but found it difficult to write poems or to get on with the 'Play for Voices'. When Dent published his *Collected Poems* on 10 November 1952 there was widespread critical acclaim, followed by voluminous sales on both sides of the Atlantic. But the terrible irony for Dylan Thomas himself was that although he was hailed by one London critic as 'the greatest living poet in English', he had only written six new poems since his last substantial publication in Britain, *Deaths and Entrances*, in 1946. On 16 December 1952, his father died, the man who had remained the greatest inspiration to the poet from his childhood.

By April 1953 Thomas was back in America, where he gave an immensely successful solo reading of the as yet unfinished *Under Milk Wood*, and later gave the first theatre presentation of the play, scribbling the final parts just before the actors, five others beside himself, went on stage. He returned to London in June, and then to Wales, to the same

*Lecture tours arranged for visiting writers or academics to speak at a series of American universities.

interacting strain of his persistent money worries and his gnawing fear of not being able to write poetry any more. Some revisions were made to the script of *Under Milk Wood*, which was finally delivered to its London producer, Douglas Cleverdon, four days before Thomas left again for America on 19 October 1953. He worked on rehearsals of *Under Milk Wood*, of which very successful stage-readings were given on the 24th and 25th of October, spoke with comic evasiveness at a film symposium on the 28th, and the next day gave a reading of poems at the City College of New York. At the same time, however, his bouts of heavy drinking were becoming more frequent, ending in maudlin self-criticism or in irrational behaviour. He had already made himself so ill that Elizabeth Reitell, his American girlfriend, insisted on his seeing a doctor on 23 October; on 4 November, claiming to have drunk eighteen straight whiskies the previous night in little over an hour, he was suffering severely from gastritis and gout. That evening he became delirious, and on 5 November he was taken in a coma to hospital, where he died four days later, never having recovered consciousness.

Paul Ferris's biography wisely avoids taking sides with either of the two opposing views about the poet's death: Margaret Taylor says he died of being Dylan Thomas, and his wife Caitlin believes that he deliberately wanted to do away with himself before he was forty; Liz Reitell, on the other hand, asserting that there was no question of his wanting to die, claims that he was killed physiologically (by alcohol), not psychologically. Although the post-mortem did not entirely confirm Miss Reitell's opinion, it did point to drink as an antecedent cause of death. Paul Ferris believes that a mistakenly large dose of morphine administered to the poet by his doctor before he was admitted to hospital may have fatally affected his breathing. Whatever the true explanation may be, the manner of his death fitted the legend which had grown up around him. What that legend obscured was that Dylan Thomas was his own worst enemy: exhibitionism and procrastination combined to sap his creative vitality. The last words anyone heard him utter were: 'After thirty-nine years this is all I've done.'

A note on the text

The length of time that elapsed between the origin of the idea and what eventually became *Under Milk Wood* has certainly at least as much to do with Thomas's dilatoriness in completing a literary project as it has to do with delays brought about by the mysterious processes of artistic gestation; but neither of these reasons is properly amenable to factual explanation. The following account of the chequered history of the text of the play is based for the most part on Douglas Cleverdon's *The Growth of Milk Wood* (Dent, London, 1969).

It was in 1932 or 1933 that Thomas first spoke of wanting to write about twenty-four hours in the life of a Welsh town or village, in miniature imitation of James Joyce's *Ulysses* (1922), a book which he very greatly admired; but it was several years before he began to think about the subject in a dramatic context. In December 1939, after taking part in a one-act farce in aid of the Red Cross at Laugharne Castle, the home of the novelist Richard Hughes, Thomas is reported as saying: 'What Laugharne needs is a play about well-known characters – and get them all to play themselves.' Three or four years later, the idea had developed into a work with the title *The Town Was Mad*, in which the individuality and eccentricity of the villagers is condemned as insane, and they are subsequently isolated in order to protect the supposedly 'sane' conformity of the rest of the world. After he had given two broadcast talks, 'Quite Early One Morning' (1944) and 'Return Journey' (1947), and had also written a documentary script for the BBC entitled 'The Londoner' (1946) – each of which in varying degrees has a bearing on *Under Milk Wood* – Thomas outlined the plot of *The Village of the Mad* (as he now called the play) to Philip Burton, then a BBC producer in Wales. But there was still no script, and it was not until 1949 or 1950 that he seriously settled down to getting one out.

At some point in late 1950 or early 1951 Thomas gave up trying to construct a plot for the play – a matter which apparently had been causing him a lot of difficulty – and turned to what Douglas Cleverdon defines as the *radio feature*, a more fluid form than that of the radio play, which Cleverdon says 'can combine any sound elements – words, music, sound effects – in any form or mixture of forms – documentary, actuality, dramatized, poetic, musico-dramatic. It has no rules determining what can or cannot be done. And although it may be in dramatic form, it has no need of a dramatic plot'. Under this greater freedom of structure, half the play was completed and sent in October 1951 to the Italian magazine *Botteghe Oscure*, edited by Marguerite Caetani, under the provisional title, *Llareggub. A Piece for Radio Perhaps*, with an urgent request for a hundred pounds in immediate payment for the complete script to cover pressing debts, and with the promise that it would be finished in two weeks' time. A year later Marguerite Caetani received a remarkable letter of apology from the poet who now promised the rest of the play for February 1953, but she had in the interim already published the incomplete script in May 1952. By May 1953, under the pressure of engagements to present the play before an audience, Thomas had greatly extended it. On 3 May he gave a solo reading at the Fogg Museum, Harvard, followed by two stage-readings, using five other actors as well as himself, on 14 and 18 May in New York. For each of these three readings additional material was being written right up to the very last moment. A record made on 14

May, and later issued by Caedmon Publishers in New York, fortunately preserves the text of the solo reading.

During his brief return to England and Wales that summer and autumn, Thomas made some revisions to the script used in May. Among other alterations, the manuscript carried changes made for the New York audiences now restored to their original wording, the poet's own production notes, and some deletions made for the solo reading he gave at Tenby Arts Club in October 1953. The copy which somewhat fortuitously finally arrived at the BBC – Thomas had left it behind in a pub – clearly showed that further extensions to the material were planned. Cleverdon prints the list found on the verso of the page containing Mr Waldo's song under the heading 'More Stuff for Actors to say'; Daniel Jones's Second Preface to the play discusses a slightly different content of proposed additional material which Thomas had shown to him, presumably during those few months before he went back to America. Further revisions to the script, made after two stage-readings on 24 and 25 October in New York, were sent, with some cuts in the text, to the French magazine *Mademoiselle*, which published an abridged version of the play in February 1954.

It is precisely because of the various revisions and additions or changes made for different audiences in solo and in stage-readings, as well as for different publications, of what in any case was always in the poet's own view an incomplete text, that there exist no less than thirteen versions of the play whose degrees of textual variation merit consideration in Douglas Cleverdon's book. From a mass of the poet's papers his literary executor, Daniel Jones, compiled a script of the play which turned out to be almost identical with that received by the BBC. Dent, London, published this text in March 1954, with a Preface by Dr Jones, and the next month New Directions, New York, published an almost identical American edition. The Dent edition was reset in 1976 and published in their Everyman paperback series with a Second Preface by Daniel Jones. It is to this edition that the page numbers refer throughout these Notes.

Part 2

Summaries

of UNDER MILK WOOD

A general summary

Under Milk Wood is about twenty-four hours in the life of a Welsh seaside village called Llareggub, from one Spring night through the next day to the following evening. The story of this small community is told by two 'Voices' who introduce the many varied characters in the play, two of whom, Captain Cat and the Reverend Eli Jenkins, also act in part as commentators on what is for them a very familiar scene. In Dylan Thomas's own words 'the town [is] laid alive before you'; and it is exactly in this sense of revealing what exists, rather than relating what happens, that the play takes its form. Since it was written especially for radio, *Under Milk Wood* does not have act and scene divisions like a stage play, but it can be divided into four roughly equal sections which for convenience may be called 'scenes', each introduced by the two 'Voices' and beginning and ending at particular points of time. Scene I ends before dawn, with Lord Cut-Glass dreaming of the sound of a clock (p. 21); scene II ends half-way through the morning, with Captain Cat's comment on the late crowing of the cock (p. 41); scene III ends half-way through the afternoon, with Polly Garter's song (p. 61); and the final scene ends with the return of night to the town.

Detailed summaries

Since there is no story (and therefore no plot structure as such) in the play, the summary for each scene merely gives its time span, indicates how the setting is evoked, and defines the patterns of behaviour and of attitude revealed in the description of the characters and in their dialogue. The Notes and Glossaries, on the other hand, are given in considerable detail because both the mood and the meaning of the play are predominantly created out of the connotations of words and their associative links in sound and in sense. Literal meanings are given only in the case of words not in common use, or where neither a dictionary definition nor the context provides sufficient information. Widely used devices, such as the transferred epithet or the noun given adjectival function, are noted only where additional effects need explanation.

Scene I: pages 1–21

The opening establishes straight away the mode of the play as a piece written for radio by the First Voice's long introductory description which repeatedly appeals to the listener's imagination both to hear and to see what is going on. Through a series of impressionistic effects and a catalogue of comic detail we are presented with a picture of the sleeping town which is vividly peopled throughout the rest of the scene by the dreams of its inhabitants. Alternating the commentary between the First and Second Voices, with the additional help at one point of the gossip of four neighbours, Dylan Thomas here introduces most of the sixty-odd characters in the play, whose subconscious preoccupations have largely to do with the two main topics: time and sexuality.

NOTES AND GLOSSARY:

Title: 'Under' means that Llareggub is situated below the lovers' wood, but at the same time it implies that what happens there controls the life of the town, 'this place of love' (p. 71). The most direct meaning of 'Milk Wood' comes from the use of the noun 'milk' as an adjective which evokes the farmland on Llareggub Hill. But since the wood is the haunt of lovers, 'milk' also carries tangential sexual connotations

[*Silence*]: this stage direction, together with the tone adopted by the First Voice at the outset, indicates the central device of conjuring up everything for the eye and ear of the audience

To begin at the beginning: the biblical echo (Genesis 1; John 1:1–5) suggests that Llareggub stands for the Garden of Eden; this pastoral theme of innocence is emphasised at several points in the play, notably by Mary Ann Sailors and by the Reverend Eli Jenkins

bible-black: introduces the concept of Welsh Puritanism, which at one level of the play's meaning acts as a foil to the comical exposure of libertinism. In the context of the opening paragraph, the repetition of 'black' and of 'blind' evokes night and darkness

hunched: the outlined shape of the wood hillside

courters'-and-rabbits' wood: the second noun modifies the first with the suggestion of multiple breeding

snouting, velvet dingles: transferred epithets; using adjectives appropriate to moles in order to describe 'dingles' compresses the meaning and creates an impressionistic effect

dumbfound: abbreviation of the adjective 'dumbfounded' (speechless); includes the meaning of the verb 'found' (discovered by the listener)

organplaying: combines the reference to a church wedding organ (linked with the image of 'aisles' in the same sentence) with a sexual innuendo

bucking ranches: the transferred epithet (from 'horses' which are evoked without being named) also carries a sexual innuendo through its link with 'wicked' and 'jollyrodgered'

jollyrodgered sea: adjective made from the noun which literally refers to a pirate's flag and colloquially refers to the penis

anthracite statues: black horses asleep standing up; the adjective, which comes from the noun which means a type of coal, briefly alludes to a wider time scale than the present, against which the play is enacted

Llareggub Hill: the first, and only, mention of the name of the town in scene I. Dylan Thomas first used this word, which is a familiar expletive spelt backwards, in 'The Burning Baby' and in 'The Orchards', both stories first published in 1936. Out of misplaced fastidiousness, the 1954 edition of the play printed 'Llaregyb'; the correct spelling was restored in 1976

bombazine: fabric of silk or cotton and worsted, often used for women's mourning clothes

butterfly choker: high winged collar

fortywinking hallelujah: dozing, to be wakened by bursts of fervour from the singing or praying congregation

four-ale: name of a public house

quiet as a domino: since a single domino cannot make the familiar clicking sound heard when several dominoes are knocked together during a game, the simile evokes an empty bar in the public house

Ocky Milkman . . . Dai Bread: these are the first two examples in the play of the Welsh habit of referring to a person by his profession or trade in order to distinguish him from others of the same surname

cockled cobbles: the cobblestones that pave the streets are convexly shaped, like cockles; the adjective also evokes the seaside town where cockles are sold

neddying: like 'trotting', earlier in the passage, this word is used as an extension of the characteristics of Donkey Street; as 'royally', in the next line, is of Coronation Street

winds gloved and folded, and dew doffed: winds, as the garment of night, obey Church manners

tumbling: the night now takes on the characteristics of the unsteady customers of the public house

coms: misprinted 'combs' in the 1954 edition, this was the commonly abbreviated form of 'combinations', an old-fashioned garment which consisted of vest and knickers, or underpants, combined. The use of this word, as with all the details given in the following three lines, points to the author's imagination being influenced by childhood memories

Thou Shalt Not: this reference to the Ten Commandments of the Bible comically juxtaposed with glasses of teeth affectionately mocks Welsh Puritanism

dickybird-watching: 'watch the dickybird' was the phrase used by early photographers to get their subjects to look at the camera

the movement and countries . . . and big seas of their dreams: the lack of order in this list of nouns conveys at once the illogicality of dreams and their central relevance

Captain Cat: a double identification: his (supposed) seafaring past, and (as Cat) his curiosity about the town as well as his detachment from it

Davy dark: 'Davy Jones's locker' means the bottom of the sea, the grave of the drowned; metaphorically, the reference here is to the dark of Captain Cat's unconscious

wishbone: the delicate, forked bone of a chicken; here the word carries two senses: that of being picked clean, and that of wish-fulfilment (with phallic innuendo)

Nantucket: a whaling seaport in Cape Cod in the United States of America, made famous by Herman Melville's (1819–91) *Moby Dick* (1851)

Duck Lane: a double sexual innuendo comes from the implication in sound of the separate substitution of 'F' for 'D', and of 'i' for 'u'

bad end, very enjoyable: this juxtaposition lightly invokes the puritan association of evil with pleasure

laverbread: laver is an edible seaweed from which in parts of Wales laverbread is made

town clock tower: phallic image

Samson-syrup-gold-maned: sweetness and strength suggested by the advertising reference to Samson on tins of golden syrup made by the firm of Tate & Lyle

Myfanwy: suggests 'my fanny', a slang expression for the vagina

Price: instead of being named by her trade, Mr Edwards's beloved is named by precisely what he is unwilling to pay

Cloth Hall of the world: like that of a character in a novel by Charles Dickens (1812–70), whose behaviour defines his profession, Mr Mog Edwards's life is totally preoccupied with drapery; only in his imagination does love take precedence over business

change hums on wires: a customer's money was sent and his bill and change returned in a small canister attached to overhead wires which ran from each counter to the cashier's office

before the mice gnaw at your bottom drawer: colloquially, a 'bottom drawer' refers to a girl's hoarding of articles in anticipation of her wedding day; metaphorically, the statement recalls Andrew Marvell's (1621–78) lines: '. . . then worms shall try/That long-preserved virginity . . .' (from 'To His Coy Mistress')

nightshirt tied to his ankles: for the sake of propriety

gooseberried: noun made into an adjective with the sense of 'gooseberry' as a fruit; and in its colloquial meaning of 'chaperon', a person who is unwanted and feels out of place in the company of lovers

tosspots: heavy drinkers

spit-and-sawdust: working-man's bar in a public house, so-called because of the sawdust-covered floor

sixpenny hops of his nightmares: Jack Black, the Puritan, is tormented by dreams of girls at the cheap local village dances

Ach y fi!: Welsh term of disgust

Evans the Death: another example of a man being named by his profession. 'Evans' was substituted for 'Thomas' in an earlier version where the author in giving his own name comically pointed up his preoccupation with death

upon waking fifty years ago: as with Captain Cat's dreams, the past lives in the present for the undertaker

welsh-cakes in the snow: a currant cake sometimes made in Wales by using snow in the mixture to give it lightness

pink-eyed: the direct reference is to the windows of the cottage lit from within; the word links with the suggestion of pig imagery in the description of Mr Waldo's size, gentleness, and appetite

dripping in the dark: 'dripping' as a noun adds to the picture of Mr Waldo's appetite; as a participle, and linked with the nursery rhyme which follows, it carries a sexual innuendo

wee wee . . .: usually the recitation of this nursery rhyme is accompanied by pulling the child's toes one by one, and then, at 'wee wee . . .', tickling him in the groin. As a child's word both for urinating and for the penis, this term here also marks the time shift in Mr Waldo's dream from his mother to his wife

Never should of married . . . If she didn't had to: colloquial syntax typical of Anglo-Welsh speech

He hasn't got a leg: an example of the idiomatic ellipsis used by the First and Second Neighbours, who comment on Waldo as a husband; and by the Third and Fourth Neighbours, who comment on Waldo as a child. Here the complete statement, 'He hasn't got a leg to stand on', means he can have no excuses for his behaviour

And seen her baby: the intonation rising sharply at the word 'seen' makes the ellipsis of 'have you seen her baby?' clear to the listener

Using language: colloquial, not exclusively Anglo-Welsh, meaning 'bad language', swearing

Singing in the w: in the 'w.c.', the lavatory (w.c. stands for water closet)

Chalking words: writing on walls: presumably obscenities, graffiti

mwchins: playing truant

b.t.m.: bottom

Lips is a penny: the time shift forward is presented here by the First Woman's voice as the introduction to a series of names which comically illustrate Mr Waldo's promiscuity

iceberg-white: links with 'holily' and 'polar' to suggest the virtuous frigidity of Mrs Ogmore-Pritchard

fume: choking smell

rinsed sleep: absurd extension of Mrs Ogmore-Pritchard's preoccupation with cleanliness

Attila: a fifth-century king of the Huns. As with Organ Morgan, the identification with the profession, here simply ironic, is made with the forename rather than the surname

got his truncheon out: to use as a conductor's baton; the idiom also carries a sexual allusion

hoofing: the image, picked up from 'cows' and from 'reindeer', adds the final unlikely event to Organ Morgan's dream: the spectacle of the prim and proper ladies of the Women's Welfare Association showing their heels and their undergarments as they dance in the moonlight

Salt Lake Farm, Mr Utah Watkins: an example of the simplest form of word transference which here carries little meaning. Salt Lake City, in Utah in the United States, is the major centre for the Mormon religion, which allows a man to take more than one wife. The implication of the following lines is that wives are as indistinguishable as sheep or as knitting stitches

foghorning: snoring associated with the policeman's booming voice of warning or command

backyard lock-up: police image for the unconscious mind

heave-ho's: sailor's term which links with 'swashes': PC Rees has used his helmet as a chamberpot

Don't spank me: suggests sexual titillation

damp pillow: specific sexual image

mogul: Lily Smalls, so named because, as Mrs Beynon's servant girl, she washes 'the smalls' (undergarments), dreams of an Eastern potentate in the washhouse; then she calls him an 'old mogul', which means, colloquially, 'you old devil' (an affectionate term for a sexual reprobate)

furnace . . . tower . . . cave . . . waterfall . . . wood . . . leap up . . . burning tall hollow splashes . . . trout: a comically exaggerated list of Freudian sexual symbols. Sigmund Freud (1856–1939) was the founder of modern psychoanalysis, related particularly to the awareness of sexuality in the unconscious mind

Inspectors of Cruelty: Royal Society for the Prevention of Cruelty to Animals

manchop: links with 'lambchop' in vowel sounds

Eisteddfodau: plural form of the name for the competitive festival of Welsh poetry and music, held annually

crwth: an old Welsh stringed instrument

pibgorn: a simple wooden pipe, or flute

druid's seedy nightie: a joke about the druid's white robes

parchs: clergymen

fathoms asleep: keeps the link between sea imagery and sleep used throughout the scene by turning the noun 'fathom' into an adverb

gippo's: colloquial for 'gypsy'. Clothespegs were made and sold by gypsies

old man: Adam. Mary Ann Sailors's dreams, unlike those of many of her neighbours, do not differ from the reality as she sees it: in scene II (p. 45) she declares, awake, that Llareggub is the 'Chosen Land'

furred: the word-link with 'Donkey Street' gives the suggestion of being comfortably smothered

Nogood Boyo: in Thomas's radio talk, 'Return Journey', the comment 'when he was a boy up to no good but the beat of his blood' carries the implication of masturbation

Lord Cut-Glass: the nickname given Dylan Thomas as a boy because of his polished English accent. In the play Lord Cut-Glass is so absurdly conscious of the passing of time that he has not time for anything else: a wry self-criticism of the author

Scene II: pages 21–41

Scene II opens at dawn with a contrast between the First Voice's evocative picture of the still sleeping town and the clichés of the 'Voice of a Guide-Book'. Captain Cat rings the town bell to rouse the inhabitants, and the various characters are introduced by the Voices' commentary, or by their own dialogue, or by blind Captain Cat who, like the listener, cannot actually see the town. By identifying the sounds of the morning, he acts as a link between the radio audience and the awaking life of Llareggub in the closing section of the scene.

NOTES AND GLOSSARY:

chapel in an oak: simple transference of suggestion from Bethesda, the name often given to a chapel in Wales, to the owl's habitat

not by druids: by stating that the place has no historical significance, the First Voice insists upon the living present

Voice of a Guide-Book: juxtaposed with the evocative yet at the same time down-to-earth picture given by the First Voice, there is the stereotyped detail of the guide-book, whose lifeless prose contains such clichés as 'backwater of life', 'salty individuality', and 'local characters'

principality: transferred from its reference to Wales, which is called a 'principality' because it has a prince, to the sky; hence, the suggestion that Llareggub is watched over by a beneficent power

morning larked and crowed: the normal function of the participle 'belling', describing the cries of animals or birds, allows for the concentration of meaning achieved by making adjectives out of the nouns 'lark' and 'crow'

eternal hill: links with the Garden of Eden allusions (pp. 1, 20 and 45); but in describing a scene of sound and movement against the unchanging hillside background, the Second Voice here re-introduces the central preoccupation of the play with Time

Gwalia: Wales; while the Reverend Eli Jenkins's poem is clearly pastiche, comically exaggerating the methods of a landscape poet such as John Dyer (1699–1757), whose 'Grongar Hill' is alluded to in the eighth verse, the purpose is not wholly mockery. The catalogue of names, particularly of the mountains in verses three and four, and of the rivers in verses five and six, exhibits in sound and rhythm a playful affection on the part of the author for the sentiments of Welsh regionalism and nationalism

morning service: suggests that the proper function of the clergyman, like that of the poet, is to praise life

treasure: a servant whom she can't do without; ironic in view of the contrast between Mrs Beynon's attitude towards Lily and Lily's toward her

Oh there's a face: in contrast to Eli Jenkins's poem, the down-to-earth self-criticism of Lily Smalls's dialogue with herself in the mirror is deliberate play-acting

conk: (*slang*) nose

I want to look *out*: at this point the listener is given Mrs Pugh's view of the town

fishwife gulls: compressed simile. This reference to the gulls' view of the town allows each of the seven characters who follow to introduce himself/herself, thus avoiding the repeated interpolation of the Voices

gypsied to kill: the noun is given an adjectival function, which adds to the meaning inferred from the colloquial phrase 'dressed to kill'

see my body: Anglo-Welsh ellipsis for 'you can see . . .'; hence, what is merely a suggestion is given the sense of an imperative

frock-coat belonged to: Anglo-Welsh ellipsis. This statement contains an element of comic self-deprecation by the author, who is identified with Lord Cut-Glass since that was his nickname as a boy. Eli Jenkins is identified with Dylan Thomas's great uncle, Gwilym Marles Thomas, who was a chapel minister and an Eisteddfod bard; the fact that Lord Cut-Glass comes into possession of Eli Jenkins's frock-coat implies that Dylan Thomas is a hand-me-down poet, that his is a second-rate talent

big-besomed: since the word echoes the more familiar term 'big-bosomed', both meanings are present

swigs: the common colloquial reference is to drinking alcohol: Mr Waldo's drinking habits are betrayed at breakfast time in a type of Dickensian caricature

back: backyard

broods: verbal image picked up from 'hens'

bubbles . . . coven: though joined alliteratively to 'broods', 'bubbles' carries a shift in meaning in connection with the collective noun 'coven' which is transferred from witches to kettles

Bread of Heaven: the hymn 'Guide me, O thou great Jehovah', sung to a famous Welsh tune, is familiarly identified by these words which are repeated in its first verse

doctored: rendered sexually neuter

shrilled off to school: the adjective made into a verb combines the effects of both

green lathered trees: seen from a distance like bubbles of green soap: an impressionistic picture

Manchester House: Manchester, the centre of the cotton industry

darkness behind his eye: in his mind; though he shouts to himself that he loves Miss Price, all that comes out is a whisper

Captain Cat hears all the morning: from this point to the end of scene II (p. 41) Captain Cat takes over most of the commentary; blind like the listener, he identifies the various sounds and introduces the characters

and a bath vegetarian: the identification of a man by his trade or profession (in this case by his habits), together with extreme ellipsis, produces this comical juxtaposition. In Anglo-Welsh speech the intonation would also help to carry the meaning that the visitor, who is a vegetarian, wants a room with the use of a bath

bang of dawn: although the substitution of 'bang' for 'crack' adds nothing to the normal sense of the idiom, the sexual allusion of 'birds' (meaning girls; scene III, p. 42) links with 'bang' (colloquial for intercourse) and 'telescope' (phallus)

a egg: Anglo-Welsh usage

paternity summons: a court order forcing the father of an illegitimate child to support it financially

High heels now: in addition to its adverbial function, 'now' in Anglo-Welsh usage conveys the understood imperative 'take note' or 'pay attention'

there should be a law: Captain Cat, unable to hear what the women are saying, imitates their gossip. This kind of fragmentary, half-stated accusation works by implied or tacitly understood meanings: the speaker exposes Polly Garter's promiscuity, but because the syntax of her statement is incomplete, she is able to pretend that such behaviour should not be talked about

wedding-ringed holy: the adjective 'holy' is given the additional function of a noun, meaning 'hole' (crowded, squalid place); hence, the normal meaning of 'holy' is turned ironically in reference to the married mothers at the dance in the Welfare Hall. The unmarried Polly Garter's virtue is that she has her babies for love's sake only

Scene III: pages 41–61

After a long descriptive passage by the First Voice, full of images of action, movement and sound, which are linked through alliteration and onomatopoeia as well as through meaning, the commentary is briefly taken over by the voices of four women who expose the foibles and misdemeanours of several townspeople in swift snippets of gossip. The First and Second Voices then resume the alternating pattern of introducing particular characters whose dialogue frequently reveals the contrast between their secret wishes and desires and the reality. For the first time songs are brought into the play – the First Voice announces that 'the morning is all singing' – and the refrain from Polly Garter's song mixed with a snatch of the refrain from the children's song is used to juxtapose innocence and experience. A sequence of stark sexual encounter in the children's game of kisses and forfeits is followed by images of unfulfilled desires in the relationship between Gossamer Beynon and Sinbad Sailors, which in turn is contrasted with the acid bickering of Mr and Mrs Pugh and the vindictive envy of Mrs Organ Morgan. The vivid preoccupation with the present which predominates throughout the scene is countered at the end by two different kinds of reference to the passing of time: Lord Cut-Glass's fear of the Day of Judgement marked by his obsession with clocks, and Polly Garter's wistful memory of her dead lover.

NOTES AND GLOSSARY:

beargarden: noun meaning a place where bears are baited (a scene of tumult), used here as an adjective

la di da: both intonation and meaning convey derision at Mrs Ogmore-Pritchard's pretensions of gentility and superiority

dead beat: exhausted; this reference to Mrs Organ Morgan's marital life is made clear by the sexual pun on the word 'organ' in the next line

martyr: specifically used later as a sexual image with reference to Polly Garter (see 'martyred' below)

there is no leg: Jack Black's attempt to drive out sensuality from his thoughts defines what form it takes in his imagination

ship: nautically, the verb means to take aboard

jig jig: international slang term for sexual intercourse

Chosen Land: biblical analogy with 'chosen people'; suggests Eden, Paradise, timelessness. Mary Ann Sailors, the oldest inhabitant of Llareggub, gives the clearest articulation of the play's theme as a pastoral idyll

Twll: the Welsh word for 'arse-hole' (pun on 'twill', a kind of worsted cloth); hence the slur on Mr Edwards's advertising in the *Twll Bugle*

Wardrobes Bought: implies that Mr Edwards does not sell much clothing

dripping wet: sexual allusion

she never got stockings: Mr Edwards's naivety about garters worn solely for sexual titillation underlines his ignorance of the sexual purport of his dream

three-seated shack: the outside lavatory

gob: (*slang*) spit

draggletail: adjective made out of noun meaning an untidy person; hence, the suggestion that the schoolyard is full of untidy children

bay: misprint for 'baby'

music of the spheres: idea of Greek origin that the planets' movements make beautiful sounds which provide celestial proof of the harmony of all things in Nature

is heard distinctly: the matter-of-fact statement about a poetic concept emphasises the irony of the next sentence

'The Rustle of Spring': the title of a sentimental piece of piano music by Sinding. The mockery of the First Voice's reference to this musical cliché is somewhat out of context with the tone of the rest of the commentary on the life of Llareggub

wall eye: a staring eye, suggesting drunkenness and/or sensuality

Tom . . . Dick . . . Harry: that is, everyone and anybody: these names declare Polly Garter's promiscuity

little Willy Wee (Weazel): child's name for penis. There may be some playful autobiographical reference here, since Dylan Thomas considered himself similarly disadvantaged sexually

Praise the Lord!: double dramatic irony in that the innocent Reverend Eli Jenkins is as unaware of Polly's sexual exploits as he is of the fact that her capacity for love actually merits the invocation

treacle: dark beer; stout

flush: alliterative effects predominate, but the literal meaning of the verb is also appropriate: the drink goes down as fast as water in a lavatory cistern, brought about by a single movement of hand and arm

soft as Eve and sharp as sciatica: antithetical similes, referring to body and mind

sciatica: a disease; by substituting this word for the usual element in the comparison (sharp as a razor), the cliché is revitalised and the meaning, given impact by the alliteration, is made more specific by comic exaggeration: a sharp-tongued woman is an affliction

ding a ding: from the refrain of a song in William Shakespeare's (1564–1616) *As You Like It* (V.iii.17–36). The interpolation of words from the children's song in Polly Garter's song about her lovers emphasises their sexual innuendo, and at the same time presents an equation between innocence and experience which is one of the play's central themes

forfeiting: a children's game in which failure to carry out a 'dare' (challenge) carries a penalty

Dirty Dick . . . rhubarb stick: the sexual implications of the rhyme come from the use of the slang name for penis ('Dick') and from the phallic image in 'rhubarb stick'

cawl: mutton broth with leeks and potatoes

bees: from a Welsh word meaning underclothes

Dai-Adamed: 'Dai', a very common first name in Wales, is often used to refer to any Welshman; linked with 'Adam' and made into an adjective, the word evokes a world peopled solely by naked Welshmen

Sinbad: the contrast of 'sin' and 'bad' with the fairytale source of the name adds to the ambivalence of the passage as a whole

mangrowing cock-crow garden: a fusion of images of sexual experience and of first beginnings and innocence

reverent goat-bearded hands: the antithesis of the religious and the lustful succinctly exposes the conflicting elements in Gossamer Beynon's imagination

salad-day: again implies Gossamer Beynon's innocence, but this time with ironic reference (see Shakespeare's *Antony and Cleopatra,* I.v.73)

cucumber: phallic symbol

hooves: symbol of sexual power

middle of the world: sexual reference

shroud: noun used as adjective, describing the meat both as dead and as covered up (that is, by the potato in the cottage pie)

jeroboams: large bottles

martyred: see note on 'martyr', above. Mrs Pugh's irony exposes her own character, not, as she intends, that of Polly Garter

stabbing: with her beak; continues the pelican image of voracious appetite and at the same time describes the nature of Mrs Organ Morgan's attack upon Polly Garter's promiscuity

loudlipped: wide-rimmed surrounds to the clock-face

Last Black Day: Day of Judgement

Armageddon Hill: site of the last battle fought between the nations before the Day of Judgement (see the Bible, Revelation 16:16)

Scene IV: pages 61–82

The last scene of the play passes from a sleepy mid-afternoon swiftly through dusk to nightfall. Among the many characters who reappear, the listener meets Captain Cat dreaming of Rosie Probert and weeping both her loss and the loss of his past; the listener is privy to the secret and sensual daydreams of Nogood Boyo and of Mae Rose Cottage (and later sees the former's wishes fulfilled in the shape of Lily Smalls in the washhouse); he hears Mrs Ogmore-Pritchard chastising her dead husbands, and listens to the simple sentiments of the Reverend Eli Jenkins's sunset poem and to Mr Waldo's lusty song in the public house. The emphasis in this scene is on the confrontation of the present with the past, of life with death; but apart from the dialogue between Captain Cat and the dead Rosie Probert, this theme is for the most part dealt with lightly and in comic terms. Its seriousness is reaffirmed at the very end of the play when the refrain of Polly Garter's song about her dead lover is poignantly set against the evocation of Milk Wood as an Eden, as a symbol of innocence, but above all as a 'place of love'.

NOTES AND GLOSSARY:

Doctor Crippen: a famous murderer who poisoned his nagging wife, cut up her body, and buried the pieces in his cellar

Black Death: a plague which swept through Europe in the fourteenth century

clippered: the noun 'clipper', a tall-masted sailing ship, is given adjectival force

blowzy-breasted dead: the description of dissipation from drink which is carried by the adjective 'blowzy' is combined with a macabre picture of the bloated bodies of the drowned

Jack: common name for a sailor; hence, all men or any man

Quack twice: the image link (Duck . . . Quack) is stressed at the expense of sense

sardined: the noun made into an adjective carries two meanings: tightly together, and innumerable

Tom Cat: implies sexual promiscuity

master . . . bosun: sea terms describing different sexual relationships between Captain Cat and Rosie Probert, the last of which ('My little deck hand', p. 65) puts the Captain in the most servile position

My pretty sugar sailor: this play on 'sugar daddy' (American slang for a wealthy old man who gives a young woman presents in return for her favours) again shifts the definition of the sexual relationship

shipwreck: along with Rosie's next statement, 'Knock twice, Jack,/At the door of my grave/And ask for Rosie', this image links sexual love with death

Is vanishing from her: the image which is used to describe the dead Rosie Probert forgetting her life on earth also starkly evokes the body in dissolution

gypsies: the verb made out of the noun suggests an alluring and illicit sexual presence

I *won't*: Mrs Dai Bread Two's illogical reply exposes Nogood Boyo's sexual advances

gusting: participle made out of the adjective 'gusty', suggesting both 'breathless' and 'full of feeling'

geisha girl: Japanese female entertainer in song and dance; sometimes wrongly used as the equivalent term for a prostitute

ricepaper: edible and partially transparent

undoes him: the context suggests masturbation

White Book of Llareggub: 'white' means virtuous, innocent; the title is also a pastiche of important Welsh manuscripts, such as *The White Book of Mabinogion*

undogcollared: dismissed from the ministry of the Church for unseemly behaviour ('dogcollar' is the familiar term for the white collar worn by parsons)

his little weakness: drink and/or sex

erect as a dry dream: the play on 'wet dream' (colloquial for ejaculation during sleep) incongruously suggests Mrs Ogmore-Pritchard's chastity

glass widow: play on 'grass-widow', suggesting both frigidity and brittle temperament

tears where their eyes once were: the echo of a line from Ariel's song from Shakespeare's *The Tempest* (I.ii.397–404), 'Those are pearls that were his eyes', gains no allusive function

Gomorrah: a sexually corrupt city (see the Bible, Genesis 18:20)

Dance of the World: sexual union which ensures the continuity of the human race

wolve and whistle: the noun 'wolf-whistle', colloquial for a rude whistle of male admiration, is split into two verbs, the first of which emphasises the animal hunting instinct in sexuality

Land of Summer: a reference to the original home of the 'Celts' (probably Southern Europe) which enjoys a better climate than that of Wales

a wife out of flowers: a direct reference to the story told in the Welsh epic, *The Mabinogion*

Come and sweep my chimbley: sexual invitation

he sees in the dark: double metaphor meaning that the town is vividly alive in Captain Cat's imagination, and that he is able to communicate with the dead

She has forgotten dying: she is in a different realm, quite removed from the condition of being human

Listen to the night breaking: we normally speak of the morning 'breaking', not the night. The normal context in which the term is used is changed, but the new context also echoes the familiar one from which it is drawn, a device frequently employed by Dylan

Thomas for merely comic effect. Here, however, because 'night' is linked with dreams of the dead, there is an additional echo from the phrase, 'the heart breaking', which evokes a serious element in the play by underlining Captain Cat's acute sense of loss

fach: the Welsh word for 'little', as a term of endearment, in its feminine form; since 'bach' is the masculine form of the word (pronounced as in 'Bach'), there is a play on the composer's name together with the suggestion that Organ Morgan's love of music supplants his love for his wife

The thin night darkens: echoes Shakespeare's *Macbeth* (III.ii.50), 'Light thickens . . .', but with opposite meaning. In *Macbeth* night is a portent of evil, whereas here it is an invitation to love-making

Milk waking Wood: 'waking' because night is the time for love

cloven: has the appearance of the Devil (from the identification of the Devil with the libertinism of the Greek God, Pan; or with the sexual appetite of the goat)

Part 3

Commentary

Form and genre

While he was trying out new directions in his poetry at the time of his death, it was through the medium of radio that Dylan Thomas planned to gain a regular professional livelihood; and although the poetry must be of primary concern in any judgement of him as an artist, it was the success of the BBC's production of *Under Milk Wood* on 25 January 1954 which assured his wider popularity. That year, in an abridged version, it won the international Italia Prize for radio, and by the end of 1955 it had been translated into over a dozen languages. In the introduction to the BBC's commemorative production in 1978, the play was described as 'a classic of radio'; and because its form is determined exactly by its genre, it is only as a radio play that it can be properly judged and performed.

The inadequacies of different sorts of adaptations of *Under Milk Wood* serve to illustrate its distinctive features as a piece for broadcasting, which has to depend entirely upon *sound* for its mood and its meaning. It has been produced for stage, film and television; but in each case difficulties arose both from the need to represent in visual terms everything which in radio is imaginatively evoked by the spoken word, and from the sheer multiplicity of characters whose constantly changing dialogue has no sequential link in any kind of narrative plot. A review in *The Times* for 22 August 1956 of the Edinburgh Festival stage production stated that the adaptation necessarily slowed down the author's conjuring tricks with words and that 'the flexible figures of the most gaily gruesome of bawdy rhetorical fancies have become stage humours and require more narrative support than they are destined to get'. The following year a critic in the same newspaper felt that the 'kaleidoscopic presentation' of a recent television production of the play robbed it of the cohesion provided by the village as an organism and 'almost made one long for a plot'. Andrew Sinclair, who wrote the screenplay for the film production, sums up the frustrations which inevitably accompany any adaptation of the play into a visual medium: 'The problem of *Under Milk Wood* as a film lay in its bittiness, cross-cutting from voice to voice all the time . . . seventy little stories to tell in ninety minutes . . . how to make the counterpoint of words into one visual whole, while being faithful to the text.'* Various devices have

*Andrew Sinclair, *Under Milk Wood* by Dylan Thomas. Screenplay by Andrew Sinclair, Lorrimer, London, 1972, p. 5.

been tried in order to get around these difficulties. In 1961 at The Lyric, Hammersmith, for example, the narration was split between two actors who sat on high stools at either side of the stage, thereby effectively diminishing the obtrusive element of visual identification; and in the Terry Hands 1968 stage production at the Aldwych Theatre, London, fluidity of action was achieved by having only seven actors doubling up parts on a very simple set. The way its first audience heard *Under Milk Wood*, in the solo reading that Dylan Thomas gave in New York on 3 May 1953, is perhaps the nearest that a stage performance can get to the play's proper medium, but it misses, of course, the advantages that radio gives of an extensive variety of voice and other sound effects.

Thomas's experience in broadcasting talks for the BBC markedly affected the form of *Under Milk Wood*, but some of its characteristics can be seen emerging several years before in the early stories. For example, 'The Orchards' (published 1936), invites the reader to share in the experience being described, as in 'poor Marlais's morning, turning to evening, spins before you . . . Marlais's death in life in the circular going down of the day that had taken no time blows again in the wind for you'. That is a long way from the First Voice's seductive affirmations of the privileges granted the listener to the radio play ('Only you can hear . . . Only you can see . . .'), but it is a hint of the same technique. When, later in 'The Orchards', Marlais stands on the hill looking down on 'the toy of the town . . . at his feet' where 'men on their errands moved to no purpose but the escape of time', there is an intimation of one of the themes of *Under Milk Wood*, as well as a similarity in its use of a detached observer of the scene, a technique which Walford Davies* also finds in the story 'Just Like Little Dogs' (from the *Portrait* collection, published in 1940). The same critic† points out that character description typical of the radio play is already present in 'The Horse's Ha' (published in 1936), in such a sentence as: 'Out came the grocer with an egg in his hand and the butcher in a bloody coat.'

But it is in the radio talk 'Quite Early One Morning', given in 1944, that the plainest early model of the play may be seen. The talk contains numerous comic details which nine years later are directly transposed into the 'Play for Voices', including Mrs Ogmore-Pritchard's nagging injunction: 'And before you let the sun in, mind he wipes his shoes.' Here the story is told in the first person, and there are no other voices until at the very end each of the seven villagers (four of whom clearly provide prototypes for characters in the radio play) recites a verse of indifferent doggerel. Neither the broadcast, 'Holiday Memory', nor the radio script 'The Londoner' (an account of a day in the life of a working-class street in the city) carries material which is directly picked up for use in the play,

*Walford Davies, *Dylan Thomas*, University of Wales Press, Cardiff, 1972, p. 69.

†Walford Davies (ed.), *Dylan Thomas: Early Prose Writings*, Dent, London, 1971, p. xv.

but each has slight similarities with the later work. In 'Return Journey' (1947), a skilful reminiscence of Swansea for which Dylan Thomas had undertaken detailed research, the poet's radio technique is much more sophisticated. The narrator in this piece not only describes the scene and introduces a varied group of characters, but also relates his own experiences and takes part in the continuing dialogue. Such a combination of the roles of actor and narrator is relatively rare in *Under Milk Wood*, but where it does occur the language used is very similar to that of the dialogue in the play. When Captain Cat takes part in the scene which he is at the same moment describing (pp. 39–40), at one point he actually imitates the conversation of the town gossips, and nowhere is his detailing of the characters' actions as richly connotative as the general introductory descriptions given by the First and Second Voices. Their narration, which is quite separate from the dialogue in the play, brings back into drama a feature which belongs to one of its earliest conventions. Greek tragedy at first largely consisted of a chorus of voices which told the audience what happened; later both chorus and actors appeared on the stage. In European drama, however, the chorus fell away and its commentary was incorporated into what the actors were to say and do. The two Voices' commentary in *Under Milk Wood* restores that additional dimension to drama which was originally supplied by the Greek chorus, but the difficulties experienced in producing Thomas's work for the stage indicate that this innovation in contemporary playwriting was more readily acceptable on the radio than in the theatre. The descriptive function of their commentary points, however, to additional influences on Dylan Thomas which were somewhat different from those solely connected with broadcasting.

Freed from the encumbrance of stage scenery as from the equally limiting actualities of TV or film cameras, the poet on radio can create a vivid scene in the listener's imagination as definite or as impressionistic as he pleases, one which he can change as swiftly as the replacement of one image in the mind by another. But since, even in the imagination, such fluidity of movement needs some kind of intelligible direction, *Under Milk Wood* opens with the First Voice giving a panoramic view of the town of Llareggub and the wood lying above it, which then closes up to the houses, and then to the people inside the houses, still asleep and inhabited with dreams. With repeated appeals to the audience to 'Look' and 'Listen', the First Voice keeps changing the focal point of the description throughout the three pages of the introduction to the play at a speed which would be far too jerky for an actual cinematographic 'panning'* of the scene. What Thomas has done here is to take over a technique from film-making and apply it in words with greater economy

*Moving a film or television camera to photograph an entire scene or follow the movement of a particular character.

than would be possible in its natural medium. That it was a very deliberate procedure on Thomas's part is made clear by J. Maclaren-Ross, who worked with the poet as a film scriptwriter during the war. In *Memoirs of the 40s* he states that the ambition he and Thomas shared was 'to write a complete scenario ready for shooting which would give the ordinary reader an absolute visual impression of the film in words and could be published as a new form of literature'.* He goes on to say that their main obstacle was to include camera directions in such a script without being too technical, and that the only examples of anything resembling what they were aiming for were to be found in *The Film Sense* by Sergei Eisenstein. The following brief sequence from 'An American Tragedy', a script which was submitted by Eisenstein to Paramount Films but rejected by that company, reveals that the changing focus of the camera and its angle of viewpoint are incorporated into the description of the scene:

> The surface of Big Bittern Lake. Pools of the inky black surface of the silent water. The dark reflection of the pines. Boats trembling on the motionless surface of the silent water. Their gunwales against a rude landing stage at the foot of the steps rising to the small hotel. The beautiful panorama of the lake . . .†

The film script for 'The Beach of Falésa', which Thomas wrote in 1948, opens in a very similar manner:

> It is the hour before tropical dawn, on the hushed, grey open sea. A boat glides by like a shadow, the moon going down behind her tall sails. The boat sails on, through the very slowly lightening night, through moonlight and music, the soft sea speaking against her sides . . . . Dawn rises, darkness drains suddenly away from the cloudless sky, and the cries of birds begin to be heard . . .‡

And the same techniques are at work in other film scripts he wrote during the same period, such as 'Me and My Bike', '20 Years A'Growing' and 'Rebecca's Daughters'. The editors' Preface to the script for 'The Doctor and the Devils' based on a notorious nineteenth-century murder trial (which, in contrast to the radio play, describes innocence destroyed by violence) shows in what direction Thomas's style was moving:

> The potential motion picture itself comes straight off the page on to a screen formed easily in the mind's eye. Yet the writing, economical, imaginative and edged with poetry, goes well beyond the boundaries

*J. Maclaren-Ross, *Memoirs of the 40s*, Ross, London, 1965, p. 129.
†Sergei Eisenstein, *The Film Sense*, Faber, London, 1943, p. 17.
‡Dylan Thomas, *The Beach of Falésa*, Stein & Day, New York, 1963, p. 7.

> of cinema . . . . [It] establishes an immediate, fully populated world of its own.*

Although he was not always able to eliminate awkward camera directions from these scripts, they all read, particularly in their openings, like sketches for *Under Milk Wood*; and they illustrate the close relationship between writing words to describe what happens in a visual medium and writing words to evoke a visual image for a medium which operates solely by means of sound.

Another parallel that can be drawn concerns the function of 'montage' in film-making, which Eisenstein defines as: 'two film pieces of any kind, placed together, [which] inevitably combine into a new concept, a new quality arising out of that juxtaposition'.† Such a 'montage' occurs in *Under Milk Wood* wherever there is a passage which does not describe an action or sequence of events but which is centrally concerned with the evocation of setting and feeling. The picture we are given, for example, of the Reverend Eli Jenkins awaking in Bethesda House is merely straightforward narrative: he 'gropes out of bed into his preacher's black, combs back his bard's white hair, forgets to wash, pads barefoot downstairs . . .' (pp. 22–3). This reveals character through action, but it does nothing else. In contrast, most of the other pieces of narration given to the First and Second Voices operate on more than one level of meaning. The simplest example of this method is perhaps the description of different sounds at the beginning of scene III, as in: 'scamper of sanderlings, curlew cry, crow caw, pigeon coo, clock strike, bull bellow, and the ragged gabble of the beargarden school . . .' (p. 41). Even in such a list of what are mostly commonplace terms, juxtaposition of the particular items creates an effect which is additional to, if not different from, what each represents. Where the poetic texture is richer than this, as is generally the case throughout the play, a new idea can be brought in by a single image, as in the opening description of night, 'starless and bible-black', which immediately suggests something else besides actual darkness (see 'bible-black', Notes and Glossary, p. 19 above). Indeed, some of Thomas's staple literary devices, such as his use of the transferred epithet or his changing of one of the terms of a familiar idiom or simile to a word which sounds almost the same but has a different meaning (see 'glass widow', for example, Notes and Glossary, p. 33 above), work to the same end of multiple connotation. In both their trivial and their serious implications, Thomas's words in *Under Milk Wood* achieve a 'montage' of sight and sound and image with a fluency no camera can possess.

In his talk 'Return Journey', Thomas had experimented with

*Dylan Thomas, *The Doctor and the Devils*, Time Life Books, New York, 1964, p. vi.
†Eisenstein, *op. cit.*, p. 16.

additional sounds such as the noise of bells or of children singing in the background, and had described whatever sound accompaniment was appropriate for his film scripts, but in the radio play he uses these effects very sparingly. The most extended sequence of background noises occurs when Captain Cat 'hears all the morning' (pp. 35–9). Elsewhere, apart from the music for the songs, which enhances mood and meaning strikingly at several points in the play, it is largely the words that do the work. And it is the way those words are pronounced, including variations both in pitch and tone and in the timing of pauses between different speakers, which controls some of the most subtle effects of the play. Although Dylan Thomas scornfully repudiated any comments about the 'Welshness' of his poetry, saying that he 'never understood this racial talk',* he did recognise that *Under Milk Wood* was best performed by Welsh voices.† Some of the ways in which Anglo-Welsh intonations clarify elliptical syntax‡ in the play are referred to in Part 2 (see, for example, the notes on 'And seen her baby' and 'la di da', pp. 23 and 29 above); but while intonation and accent are particularly marked in the swift passages of dialogue which are more like choruses of various voices (see scene I, pp. 3–5; scene II, pp. 33–4; scene III, pp. 41–3), such influences are impossible to analyse fully without illustrations from a recording by Welsh actors and actresses. It is a commonplace of dramatic criticism that we must take into account action as well as words, that we must think of a play as a performance on the stage – not just as a reading text. But merely to read a play written specifically for broadcasting presents us with the much greater problem of imagining how it should sound. One of the most daunting tasks facing a translator of *Under Milk Wood* must be that of finding equivalents in tone as well as in image and meaning for its words, which further underlines the distinctiveness of the form and genre of the play. The last word in its original title, *Llareggub. A Piece for Radio Perhaps*, was a perfectly unnecessary qualification.

Themes

The idea of a community cut off from the rest of the country was part of the original format of the play under its title *The Town Was Mad*, but at this stage the isolation was to have been the result of the trial of the inhabitants by representatives of the supposedly 'sane' world outside. In *Under Milk Wood* Thomas dropped this plot and with it any concern for dramatic conflict between right and wrong, vice and virtue. Since there is no reference to any kind of moral code governing the behaviour of the

*Quoted in the *Times Literary Supplement*, 2 March 1957.

†J. M. Brinnin, *Dylan Thomas in America*, Dent, London, 1956, pp. 155–6.

‡Where the grammar of a sentence is incomplete but understood.

characters in the play, and therefore no invitation to the listener to pass judgement upon them, the closest tradition to which *Under Milk Wood* may be seen to belong is that of Arcadia, the literary expression of a rustic paradise which goes back to the Greeks and Romans. When Thomas sent the first half of the script to the magazine *Botteghe Oscure* in 1951, he gave a lengthy description of the play which ends with a justification of his characters' eccentricities. Mary Ann Sailors, the author says:

> is not all mad: she merely believes in heaven on earth. And so with all of them . . . all, by their own rights, are ordinary and good; and the 1st Voice, and the poet preacher, never judge nor condemn but explain and make strangely simple and simply strange.*

Of course, Thomas's Arcadia is in the context of a Christian, not a Greek civilisation, and so his images of innocence are primarily couched in familiar biblical terms. As we have already seen (Notes and Glossary, p. 19 above), the opening words, 'To begin at the beginning', link with Mary Ann Sailors's view of the town as the 'Chosen Land' (p. 20 and p. 45) and with the Reverend Eli Jenkins, who records its genealogical virtue in the 'White Book of Llareggub' (p. 68), where the history of the most inconsequential of its inhabitants, the gentle simpleton, Bessie Bighead, is 'laid out . . . with as much love and care as the lock of hair of a first lost love' (p. 70).

The play's evocation of ideal innocence is protected from the dangers of sentimentality by a pervasive comic parody which operates as much through sound as through meaning. But it does not operate in the same way for every character: the extent of the parody employed in the portrait of a particular individual helps to define the author's attitude towards him. For example, apart from the juxtaposition of Mary Ann Sailors's appearance in the play with comic events or characters (as when we hear Organ Morgan snoring while she dreams of Eden, p. 20), the portrait of her innocence is benignly free of irony or parody, whereas that of the Reverend Eli Jenkins is affectionately mocking, as in the picture of his love for his village and for his native land (pp. 23–4 and p. 73). Because at the age of eighty-five she is the oldest person in the village, Mary Ann Sailors's belief in a heaven on earth does, however, cast some irony upon the activities of those characters who, consciously or not, show painful awareness of the passing of time. The Reverend Eli Jenkins matches her in his sermons of praise to what exists, to what is; and in this dimension the theme of Thomas's play parallels that of his poetry – except, of course, that the listener is made to smile at the

***Botteghe Oscure*, ed. Marguerite Caetani, Rome, vol. XIII, 1953, p. 96. (Thomas's letter to Madame Caetani is dated October 1951.)

preacher's simplicity of viewpoint. Yet this is an indulgent smile, perhaps even an envious one. At the very end of the play the only note which is out of harmony with the lovers, with Mary Ann Sailors's and Eli Jenkins's view of life, and with Spring itself in the 'Milk Waking Wood', is the reference to Jack Black, who sees the devil in every tree. But the fact that he does so merely emphasises the absurdity of any concept other than that of an idyll of innocence and love.

To cite such things as the enmity of Mr and Mrs Pugh or the loose-living of Polly Garter as contradicting such a theme is groundless, because the very tradition to which the play belongs allows for realistic treatment of human nature. What is perhaps the most famous of all literary Arcadias, Shakespeare's *As You Like It*, contains the most rationally outspoken of his heroines; and the pastoral tradition, to which both that play and Thomas's belong, has its roots in the highly realistic *Idylls* of the Greek poet Theocritus (*c*.310–*c*.250BC). But there is little need of literary precedent to justify the kind of lives Thomas's characters live in *Under Milk Wood*. Although what he explains about them in his letter to *Botteghe Oscure* has nothing to do with morality – nor should it have, given his purpose in writing the play – it does have to do with recognisable human characteristics. Mog Edwards and Miss Price write love letters to each other every day but never speak, because they prefer to keep passion at a distance; Dai Bread's two wives live in a love-hate relationship, as do Mr and Mrs Pugh, whose marriage allows their respective needs to plot and to nag complete freedom of action. As Thomas says, 'He would always like plotting, whoever he lived with; she would always like nagging, whoever she lived with. How lucky they are to be married'.* None of the characters stands accused for eccentricities, whatever form they take; and the statement, 'There's a nasty lot live here when you come to think' (p. 42), is completely disarmed of its pejorative meaning by the sequence of rapid commentary in which it occurs, which is comically exaggerated almost to the point of surrealism:

SECOND WOMAN
she said Butcher Beynon put dogs in the mincer
FIRST WOMAN
go on, he's pulling her leg
THIRD WOMAN
now don't tell her that, there's a dear
SECOND WOMAN
or she'll think he's trying to pull it off and eat it.
FOURTH WOMAN
There's a nasty lot live here when you come to think.

**ibid.*, p. 95.

On the other hand, Polly Garter contributes to the play's theme at two different levels of meaning. Thomas's letter to *Botteghe Oscure* describes her as having 'many illegitimate babies because she loves babies but does not want only one man's';* and in the play it is clear that she is intended to represent a kind of sexual ingenuousness which is unassailable by the townswomen's jealous gossip. She sings about the '*good* bad boys from the lonely farms' (p. 61) in whose arms she will lie before sunset, in terms which are echoed later in Eli Jenkins's artless prayer, 'We are not wholly bad or good/Who live our lives under Milk Wood . . .' (p. 73). But Polly Garter's comment, 'Oh, isn't life a terrible thing, thank God?' (p. 29), brings up an aspect of the confrontation of innocence and experience which is more poignant than it is comic, and which is concerned with Time and Loss and Death. And although such seriousness is nearly always deflated or modified by various forms of comedy, yet in a sense Thomas's radio play exposes one of the preoccupations of his poetry, where love and sexuality are embraced as the counter-force to death.

The most light-hearted treatment of Time occurs in scene I, in the midst of the characters' dreams: Evans the Death, asleep, is re-living a morning fifty years ago (p. 7); and Mr Waldo shifts in his dream from being a child to being married and the subject of neighbours' gossip, then to the present, as widower Waldo; then back to his childhood and forward again to a present which is cheek-by-jowl with the past (pp. 8–13). Scene I closes with Lord Cut-Glass inanely imitating a clock; but when we get to the end of scene III, the description of his kitchen containing sixty-six clocks, all set at different hours, goes beyond the merely comic: the absurd exaggeration tells of Lord Cut-Glass's terror of time. Living in fear that the end of the world will come before he knows it, he presents a direct contrast to Mary Ann Sailors, who joys in 'Spring in Llareggub in the sun in [her] old age' (p. 45). Although she knows exactly how old she is, she acts as if present, past and future were indistinguishable.

Wherever reference to the concept of Time in the play also evokes that of Loss and of Death, the comic tone is frequently modified, and in places temporarily effaced by an awareness of the frailty of life and the fragility of dreams. The BBC's most recent production of *Under Milk Wood* amplifies this theme by interpolating a note of loss three times within the opening introduction. At the end of the first and second paragraphs and at line 7 on page 3, the ghostly voice of Polly Garter is heard repeating the last three words of the lines which act as a refrain to her song:

But I always think as we tumble into bed
Of little Willy Wee who is dead, dead, dead . . .

**ibid.*, p. 95.

This echo establishes a parallel with the theme expressed throughout the play by its main character, Captain Cat, who seeks to defeat Time by re-living the past in the present. Other than those of the commentators, the first voices we hear come from Captain Cat's drowned companions who appear to him in his dreams. The sequence is comic because of the rapidity, brevity, and banality of the exchanges; but at the same time, the dead sailors' past is shown still vividly alive in them. At the very end of the play their voices are heard again when we are informed (p. 77) that Captain Cat can see into the past because:

> Like a cat,
> he sees in the dark. Through the voyages of his tears
> he sails to see the dead.

Earlier, his dialogue at the beginning of scene IV (pp. 63–6) with the ghost of Rosie Probert, the prostitute who was his sweetheart, yields a similar quality of compassion at its close. After the powerful image linking dissolution and the obliteration of memory, 'The earth which filled her mouth/Is vanishing from her', Captain Cat hopelessly calls out, 'Come back, come back', a cry which is first heard in Thomas's story, 'A Prospect of the Sea', published in 1937. The lament for lost happiness is a dominant theme throughout his work, best remembered perhaps from his poem, 'Fern Hill'; but in the poem as in the play, the sense of loss is assuaged by memories of the past which exist in the present. Because such memories in the play occur for the most part in the realms of sleep (a notable exception being Polly Garter's song), there is a sense in which the wish-fulfilment of the subconscious is set against the shortcomings and frustrations of everyday existence. But this opposition is resolved when night falls on the town again, and we are told that 'the suddenly wind-shaken wood springs awake for the second dark time this one Spring day'. The wood is awake because it is the place of lovers as well as of dreams; in idealising the former and giving plausibility to the latter, Dylan Thomas has created a community which, although it is based on recognisable elements of human experience, is kept at a distance from reality.

It would be a gross distortion to interpret the play as a whole in serious terms, for at no point is any reference made to Time, Loss and Death without an accompanying or immediately subsequent deflating of its meaning by comic contrast. No attempt is made at a sustained exploration of the nature of the human condition, and it would be equally irrelevant to look for such a theme as to criticise the play for not having it. Trivial and absurd, comic and endearing, at times touching and poignant, it is never a world of embattled moral values. What it stands for is innocence, but an innocence suffused with a parody which is sometimes very down-to-earth, sometimes affectionate, and sometimes wryly apt, as when the words of the children's song (from Shakespeare's *As You Like It*) fit into Polly Garter's chorus (p. 52):

CHILDREN'S VOICES
When birds do sing hey ding a ding a ding
Sweet lovers love the Spring . . .
SECOND VOICE
Polly Garter sings, still on her knees,
POLLY GARTER
Tom Dick and Harry were three fine men
And I'll never have such
CHILDREN
ding a ding
POLLY GARTER
again

The sexual allusion here is rendered inoffensive precisely by the listener's recognition that, for all her experience, Polly Garter is as innocent as the children themselves.

Characters

Because there is no plot in the play, and therefore no conflict in external or psychological action, the characters do not change or develop. The ludicrous exaggeration of physical or mental attitudes which vividly distinguishes each personality does have a source, if in some cases a tenuous one, in real behaviour; but the comedy is too pointed and particularised for Thomas's men and women to be seen, like those of Geoffrey Chaucer's (1345–1400) *General Prologue* to the *Canterbury Tales*, as representing universal types. As with the structure of the play as a whole, which sets night against day and dreams against waking life, the characters are introduced in contrast to one another. The simple techniques of contrast and exaggeration, staples of comic presentation, form the basis of Thomas's method.

First and Second Voices

These Voices, which provide the commentary for the listening audience but do not take part in the play, function in two ways: they introduce the four scenes and indicate the passage of time between each of them; and they alternate, though not in any strictly regular order, in describing and commenting on the different characters. The First Voice does most of the work, while the Second Voice is used to provide a variation in sound and pace which at the same time helps to indicate shifts of focus or of subject in the narration. In the BBC's 1978 production, these changes were further emphasised by a more frequent alternation between the Voices, male as against female for greater contrast, than is provided for in the text.

Captain Cat

Captain Cat acts as an additional commentator in the play, but his detachment from the other characters is different from that of the First and Second Voices. In the first place, because he also takes part in what happens, his response is more subjective than theirs; and because, being blind, he has to identify the scene before him solely by means of the sounds he hears, he provides a model guide for the listening audience. Secondly, as an intimate member of the community, he characterises the individuals in it familiarly, in terms which are much more wittily conversational than is generally the case with the language used by the two Voices; and while his comments frequently carry a sharp edge of caricature ('back she goes to the kitchen', he says of Mrs Ogmore-Pritchard, 'to polish the potatoes', p. 37), they are at the same time tolerantly affectionate.

His love for the children of Llareggub is shown by the details he gives of their backgrounds and habits ('Billy Swansea with the dog's voice, one of Mr Waldo's, nasty Humphrey, Jackie with the sniff . . .', p. 35) and by his knowledge of their songs, the words of which he murmurs to himself as they sing (pp. 47–8). His identification with the children in the daytime (scenes II and III) and with the voices of the dead in his sleep at the beginning and end of the play (pp. 3–5; pp. 77–8) is not only a link between the present and the past: because in his dreams the dead are as alive to him as are the noisy children in the schoolyard opposite his house, the concept of time appears to be non-existent. The portrait of Captain Cat is used to stress a central theme in the play (see p. 44 above) which argues against the power of time to defeat and destroy. In a similar fashion, an apparent contradiction in the Captain's wayward private history is used to underline the theme of innocence. For him it was possible to be promiscuous and remain faithful in love: Rosie Probert, the girl he once shared with Tom-Fred the donkeyman and whose name is tattooed on his belly, 'is the one love of his sea-life that was sardined with women'. (p. 64). His promiscuity may have induced his blindness, as drink (it is implied) produced his red nose, but he has come through all his racy adventures unsullied in the soul. Although he is based upon the stock romantic figure of the retired sea-captain, he is the fullest character in the play, not only because of the different and very important functions he performs with reference to commentary and theme but also because of his energy, his humour, and his generous humanity.

The Reverend Eli Jenkins

He is the one other character who also acts as a commentator on the life of the town of which he is a part, but his is a different stance from that of Captain Cat, and one that presents a more subtle problem of interpretation. It is the nature of the parody involved in the depiction of this character which principally determines the author's meaning. For this gentle, ageing, absent-minded patriot and sentimentalist, poetry largely takes the place of religion. We first meet him giving his morning service of praise to Llareggub with a series of quatrains whose clever pastiche of an eighteenth-century Welsh poet's work (a clue to Thomas's source in John Dyer's (1699–1757) poem 'Grongar Hill' is given in the penultimate stanza) shows the author's playful affection for his character's love of Wales and of his familiar part of it.

The comedy is as effective in sound as in meaning when Llareggub Hill is mentioned alongside the names of famous Welsh mountains, or when the local river, the Dewi, is listed (p. 23) after the following:

By Sawdde, Senny, Dovey, Dee
Edw, Eden, Aled, all,
Taff and Towy broad and free,
Llyfnant with its waterfall . . .

Nonetheless, genuine feeling is never entirely absent from the parody; it re-emerges quite clearly at the end, despite the doggerel form of the verses, because when the Reverend Eli Jenkins says he wants to 'hear the Dewi sing all day/And never, never leave the town' (p. 24), he not only evokes Welsh regional sympathies: his meaning touches, however lightly, on the more universal themes of the play concerning time and mortality. In contrast, his last poem works on only one level of feeling and is consequently more vapid in its effect. Equally sentimental as the earlier poem but lacking its leavening of pastiche and comic exaggeration, this set of lame verses merely exemplifies the simplicity of the Reverend Eli Jenkins's view of life and death. But there is a charm in the artlessness of its prayers which saves it from the merely banal:

We are not wholly bad or good
Who live our lives under Milk Wood,
And Thou, I know, wilt be the first
To see our best side, not our worst. (p. 73)

One Welsh critic* has spoken of the assent and approval these sentiments gained from a performance in Wales; and it is clear that while no audience could misunderstand Thomas's vigorous portrait of

*John Ackerman, *Dylan Thomas: His Life and Work*, Oxford University Press, London, 1964, p. 177.

Captain Cat (see, for example, the splendid verses of his exchange with the dead Rosie Probert, pp. 64–6), that of the poet-preacher has to do with Welsh identities in sentiment and tradition: with the simple emotion of non-conformist hymnals, and with the bards of the Eisteddfodau. The last words he speaks (p. 76) draw upon two other sources of Welsh racial consciousness with little sense of parody whatsoever. Walford Davies points out* that the first part of this speech, from 'Llareggub Hill' to 'the Land of Summer', is a direct transposition from a well-known expression of Celtic romanticism found in Arthur Machen's autobiography *Far Off Things*, published in 1922; and the remaining words echo a famous passage in the Welsh epic, *The Mabinogion*, which the poet W. B. Yeats refers to as evidence for 'The Celtic Element in Literature.'† If Thomas kindly mocks the Reverend Eli Jenkins in this play, he is also mocking himself just a little, and his own ancestry. The link between poet and preacher is praise of life, which is also innocence: 'Llareggub's Land . . . [is] a greenleaved sermon on the innocence of men . . .' (p. 80).

Sequence of Voices

This device provides yet another kind of commentary for the listener, which operates in two different ways. Of the four sequences of voices (the drowned sailors, pp. 3–6 and p. 78; the four neighbours, pp. 9–12; the four women, pp. 41–3; and the children, pp. 52–5), the first and last take part in what happens in the play and at the same time underline two of its basic themes: the dead sailors' voices in Captain Cat's dreams represent his subconscious awareness of the past in the present; and those of the children act out in rhyming games the conscious force of sexual attraction. The separate sequences of neighbours' and of women's voices, on the other hand, operate as a chorus which reports on the play's action but which is less objective and more comic than the commentary of the First and Second Voices because it is delivered in the rapid exchange of idiomatic gossip.

Rosie Probert

The voice of the dead Rosie Probert is heard on page 4 and again on page 78 among those of the dead sailors who people Captain Cat's dreams. Although she is the port prostitute – 'In that gulf and haven, fleets by the dozen have anchored for the little heaven of the night' (p. 63) – her promiscuity is not shown as sordid or reprehensible. She is seen as satisfying a natural need; but at the same time, because Captain Cat

*Walford Davies, *Dylan Thomas*, University of Wales Press, Cardiff, 1972, p. 4.
†W. B. Yeats, *Essays and Introductions*, Macmillan, London, 1961, p. 176.

loved her and because her ghost chooses him alone to speak to, out of all those who were intimate with her, she underlines the play's theme of innocence. Her most extended dialogue with the Captain (pp. 64–6) ends on a poignant contrast between life (pictured in seafaring and sexuality) and death (pictured in earth and oblivion).

Mog Edwards and Myfanwy Price

The proprietor of Manchester House is too preoccupied with his drapery business, and the seamstress/sweetshop owner too particular about the orderliness of her existence (p. 28 and p. 55) for there to be any possibility of a union between them. Speaking of 'their odd and once it is made clear, most natural love', Thomas says:

> Every day of the week they write love letters to each other, he from the top, she from the bottom, of the town: all their lives they have known of each other's existence, and of their mutual love: they have seen each other a thousand times, and never spoken: easily they could have been together, married, had children: but that is not the life for them: their passionate love, at just this distance, is all they need.*

The pair are able to preserve their dreams of wild passion precisely by preventing the changes that in reality might be brought about by its consummation. Thomas is suggesting here that for some people love may fare best when left purely to the imagination, but he is not being cynical about such an observation. This is made clear by juxtaposing the naive eroticism of Mog Edwards's letter to Miss Price with its printed heading (p. 45), and with Mrs Willy Nilly's closing comment: 'And then a little message with a rubber stamp. Shop at Mog's!!!' (p. 46).

Jack Black

At the opposite pole to Polly Garter, the portrait of the cobbler Jack Black exposes the repressive forces of Welsh Puritanism. His resistance to any form of sexual enjoyment is seen not only as savage, meaning intense and uncivilised (p. 7), but also as both furtive and perverted. His nightshirt is tied to his ankles (p. 7), the flies of his 'religious trousers' are sewn up with thread (p. 73), and the way he goes about trying to banish sensuality from his own thoughts demonstrates the futility of the attempt (p. 44). Furthermore, when he hunts down lovers in Milk Wood, his zeal is corrupted by his pleasure as he sets out 'torched and bibled, grimly, joyfully, into the already sinning dusk' (p. 73). Because night for him is synonymous with sin, he represents an absurd contrast by which the theme of innocence and love is in part defined.

**Botteghe Oscure*, ed. Marguerite Caetani, Rome, 1953, vol. XIII, p. 95.

Mr Waldo

There is nothing secretive or self-deluding about Mr Waldo's attitude to food, drink and women; these appetites are part of his nature, and the fact that he has a gentle, if self-indulgent, disposition (see the description of his bedroom, p. 8) pre-determines our view of them. As his dreams show, Mr Waldo's natural response to sexuality is badgered and beleaguered by bargaining women and by a legalistic religion. The little girl, Matti Richards, demands a penny for a kiss from Waldo the boy, just as the grown-up Waldo has to pay for his pleasure (p. 12); and when his various women, including his wife, are brought in his dream to the altar, it is the boy Waldo who screams against such constraints on his freedom (pp. 12–13). While his mother and his wife worry about what others may say, the chorus of censorious neighbours' comments on his misdemeanours both as a child and as an adult is not without a hint of envy, or even grudging admiration; but as the male counterpart of Rosie Probert and Polly Garter, his representation of the natural forces of propagation is inevitably more robust and roguish than theirs, as is witnessed in the vigour and suggestiveness of his song in the public house at the end of the play (pp. 76–7). Although this Jack of a number of not quite respectable trades – 'rabbitcatcher, barber, herbalist, cat-doctor, quack' (p. 8) – presumably receives even more paternity summonses now that he is a widower, his promiscuity is not morally condemned in any way. Mrs Pugh's sanctimonious comment, 'Saint Polly Garter . . . was martyred again last night. Mrs Organ Morgan saw her with Mr Waldo' (p. 59), is of course meant ironically; but the listener accepts the link, and it is Mrs Pugh, not Polly Garter nor Mr Waldo, who is diminished by the statement.

Mrs Ogmore-Pritchard

Obsessed with hygiene and health foods, Mrs Ogmore-Pritchard drove her second husband to an ironic death which was caused by his drinking disinfectant; and it is implied that her first husband, Mr Ogmore, was led into voyeurism and to hang his dog because of her intrepid fastidiousness (p. 42). Although in her dreams her husbands' ghosts repeat like a litany her rules of behaviour (pp. 13–15), they respond with terror and horror to the 'acid love in her voice' and plot together 'the loveless destruction of their glass widow' (p. 71). The way her bossiness and her preoccupation with cleanliness work against nature is indicated by the mocking commentary of the women's voices (pp. 41–2) and by Captain Cat's epigrammatic witticism: 'That old Bessie would beeswax the lawn to make the birds slip' (p. 36).

Gossamer Beynon and her parents

The schoolteacher daughter of the butcher and his wife has erotic dreams both at night and in the daytime (p. 15 and p. 56) which are totally at variance with her actual conduct, 'demure and proud and schoolmarm . . . the butcher's unmelting icemaiden' (pp. 56–7), and with her concern for refinement (p. 44). Her father has a reputation as a bit of a wag – he even plays tricks with his own dreams (p. 18) – and his wife provides a perfect subject for his tales because she never appears to realise that he is always pulling her leg. He baits her to the point of hysteria in an 'everymorning hullabaloo' (p. 32) which they both enjoy. But there is also a sense in which the macabre surrealism of the opening description of him, 'Mr Beynon, in butcher's bloodied apron, spring-heels down Coronation Street, a finger, not his own, in his mouth' (p. 18), is never quite dispelled from the jokes about what is sold in the shop ('owlmeat, dogs' eyes, manchop', p. 18) or what is eaten at table ('Yesterday we had mole', p. 33) because Mrs Beynon believes everything her husband says.

Mr and Mrs Organ Morgan

Mrs Morgan does all the work in their general shop, which stocks everything from custard to hatchets (p. 41), while her husband spends most of his time playing the organ in the chapel. She is not self-righteously contemptuous of promiscuity like Mrs Pugh, and clearly envies the ease with which Polly Garter keeps on producing babies (p. 59). Mrs Morgan's frustrated motherhood is further suggested by the comparison of her eating habits with those of a pelican, a bird whose capacious beak enables it to provide plentifully for its young (p. 59 and p. 60). Mr Organ Morgan takes no interest in children at all; his imagination is so dominated by music that he mistakes the drunken Cherry Owen, resting on a tombstone, for his favourite composer, the long-dead Johann Sebastian Bach (1685–1750), whom he addresses in terms of endearment (see 'fach', Notes and Glossary, p. 34 above). This fondly satirical view of the Welsh love of music is sharpened somewhat by the suggestive play upon Mr Morgan's first name made by the mocking chorus of women's voices, 'it's organ organ all the time with him', which is followed by Mrs Morgan's naive admission, 'Oh, I'm a martyr to music.' (p. 43).

Mr and Mrs Utah Watkins

The farmer and his wife, who live on Salt Lake Farm on the hill above the town, provide another contrast which in part ridicules a stereotype, in this case that of the amiably docile woman who is barely distinguishable from the sheep in the field and of her constantly complaining husband whose curses paradoxically mark his attachment to his job (pp. 69–70).

Bessie Bighead

A simpleton, born in the workhouse and left wrapped in paper on a doorstep, the Watkins's hired help is given a special place in the Reverend Eli Jenkins's White Book of Llareggub because she represents an unimpeded link between the human and the natural world. Images of holiness and light are used to describe her simplicity and gentleness (p. 70); and the irony that Gomer Owen only kissed her in the pigsty for a dare does not mock her fidelity to his memory as she decks his grave with daisies: it merely provides a touch of realism for this most basic embodiment of Thomas's Arcadia.

Mr and Mrs Willy Nilly

Unlike those of most of the other inhabitants of the town, the postman Willy Nilly's dreams (p. 17) are a pale parallel of his daytime existence, which is made constantly eventful by his reading everyone's letters. In their 'dark and sizzling damp tea-coated misty pygmy kitchen' several kettles are always on the boil for steaming open the mail and for making strong black tea which they both drink all day long and feed the slops to the 'drugged, bedraggled hens at the back door' (p. 45). Bandy-legged because he is always taking a ride out of other people's personal activities, whether they like it or not (hence his name), Willy Nilly provides the play with a minor commentary within a commentary when Captain Cat 'hears all the morning' and describes how the postman goes from door to door relaying news of their private affairs to different individuals before they open their own letters (pp. 36–9). We last see him as he 'jockeys' out to the three-seated lavatory called the House of Commons (the only political joke in the play), from which vantage point the Second Voice describes the mid-morning scene before him (p. 46).

Lily Smalls and Mae Rose Cottage

Both these young girls dream of romantic lovers, but Lily Smalls, Mrs Beynon's servant, is the more down-to-earth of the two, as can be seen from her ability to look at herself with comic objectivity (p. 25); she may dream of 'royalty who all night long went larking with her full of sauce in the Milk Wood dark' (p. 24), but she knows she has to make do with what is available, and in the end is 'up to Nogood Boyo in the washhouse' (p. 74). Mae Rose Cottage's virgin sensuality expresses itself in a pack of Freudian symbols (p. 17); and, looking after the goats in the clover (natural, as opposed to psychological symbols of procreation), she relieves her frustration by imagining that she is already notorious and damned for her sexual exploits. Drawing circles of lipstick round her nipples, she tells the goats, 'You just wait. I'll sin till I blow up!' (p. 72).

Mr and Mrs Pugh

The schoolmaster's plots against his nagging wife are presented in the traditional modes of comic deception: exaggeration, contrast, and transparent subterfuge. When Mr Pugh brings his wife her morning cup of tea (p. 26) he whispers to himself:

> Here's your arsenic, dear.
> And your weedkiller biscuit.
> I've throttled your parakeet,
> I've spat in the vases.
> I've put cheese in the mouseholes.

And then, entering the bedroom:

> Here's your . . .
> . . . nice tea, dear.

Later, having remembered ground glass as he juggled his omelet (p. 29), Mr Pugh delights in fantastically detailing in his imagination the various means by which he could poison her, including:

> a venomous porridge unknown to toxicologists which will scald and viper through her until her ears fall off like figs, her toes grow big and black as balloons, and steam comes screaming out of her navel. (p. 58)

The whole town knows, via Willy Nilly (who says it is 'small news'), that Mr Pugh has 'bought a book on how to do in Mrs Pugh' (p. 38) – the whole town, that is, except Mrs Pugh herself. It would not do, of course, for her to find out his 'secret', any more than he would actually welcome a change in her nagging, 'sweet as a razor' attitude towards him. It is not a marriage of physical union – a point surrealistically indicated by the scene of their encounters being described as a kind of mortuary where Mr Pugh 'forks the shroud meat in' (p. 57) – but of perpetual mental feud, a mock battle which they both enjoy. So that he can continue to pose as Dr Crippen, she must remain 'his needling stalactite hag and bednag of a pokerbacked nutcracker wife' (pp. 62–3).

Mary Ann Sailors and Sinbad

The character of Mary Ann Sailors reflects themes concerning Innocence and Time in the play (see pp. 41–2 and p. 43 above). Her dreams of the past in the present (p. 20) evoke a picture of the Garden of Eden, which in the daytime she identifies as Llareggub, the 'Chosen Land' (p. 45), the 'God-built garden' (p. 79) she has never left since her birth eighty-five years ago. The clock in the Sailors Arms, where Sinbad lives with his grandmother and acts as barman, has been stopped for fifty years at opening time, which suggests the happy freedom from outside laws and regulations enjoyed in the town. But while Mary Ann Sailors rejoices in Spring in her old age (p. 45), Sinbad is tormented by it because it awakens his love for Gossamer Beynon. In contrast to Captain Cat and Mr Waldo, Sinbad has never been to sea and has no experience with women. More seriously, in contrast with his grandmother he is self-centred in wanting her to die so that he can own the pub (p. 52), and he seems totally to lack her powers of imagination. It is Gossamer Beynon's erotic dreams of their frustrated love which we hear, not his (whereas in the Mog Edwards/Myfanwy Price relationship these roles are reversed); but his timidity is in part brought about by the 'educated' air which she cultivates, a class distinction which, though lightly dealt with in the play, rings true to life.

Dai Bread and his wives

Dai Bread appears only briefly, once dreaming of harems (p. 21) and again in the morning as he rushes off to the bakery (pp. 27–8). Much more detail is given of his two wives: the one, plump and comfortable, a straightforwardly mothering, if rather simple lady; and the other, slinky and gaudily alluring, a dark-bodied gypsy (p. 28). Apparently, Dai Bread has quite enough energy to satisfy both (p. 49), but the extreme contrast between them suggests that a combination of what each represents for him could never be found in one woman, and that therefore polygamy not only works but may well be necessary for some people in 'this place of love' (p. 71).

Lord Cut-Glass

For the biographical significance of this name, see Notes and Glossary, p. 25 and p. 27 above; and for the contrast to Mary Ann Sailors which his character represents, see under *Themes*, p. 43. Because, in dread fear of time, Lord Cut-Glass 'lives in a house and a life at siege' (p. 61), in contrast the strong implication to be drawn from most of the other characters in the play is that only by living fully – whether one's energies are preoccupied by frustration, bickering, dreaming of the past, having babies, making love, or merely singing praises to the blessedness of existence – can Time be overthrown. Lord Cut-Glass's insanity is his only protection; otherwise, he would be lord over nothing at all, except – to interpolate a biographical inference – his polished accent.

Polly Garter

The words that Polly Garter puts into the mouth of her latest baby, 'you're no better than you should be, Polly, and that's good enough for me' (p. 29), epitomise the amoral world of the play. What matters is the vitality of a particular relationship, not its judgement or condemnation; and in this case, of course, the link between mother and child is both natural and innocent. Polly Garter's very next statement, 'Oh, isn't life a terrible thing, thank God?', confronts innocence with those themes relating to Time, Loss and Death which are most acutely presented by the dreams of Captain Cat and by her own song, which is sung with nicely appropriate irony as she scrubs the floors of the Welfare Hall for the Mother's Union Social Dance (see 'wedding-ringed holy', Notes and Glossary, p. 28 above).

Nogood Boyo

Instead of 'Nothing' (p. 21), three of the alternative versions of the play give Nogood Boyo's first words (in which he says what his dreams are about) as, 'Turkish girls. Horizontal.'* The latter, more graphic, description better fits his main preoccupation with sexuality. He tries to bribe a little girl with three pennies; and, solely in his imagination, offers Mrs Daid Bread Two an old corset and an apple (pp. 66–7), a combination which exposes his inexperience as a lady's man and mocks the role of sex as the Satanic temptation to evil. He only makes a pretence at fishing, and in search of a meaning for his existence his mind journeys no farther than the hill he can see from the bottom of his boat (pp. 34–5). But, while he is thus seen as a natural child of Llareggub's Land, he also conveys a realistic picture of the inertia which paradoxically accompanies sexual adolescence. His fantasies are as readily evoked as they are swiftly effective (pp. 67–8), but our last view of him with Lily Smalls (p. 74) hints that they may no longer be needed.

Mr and Mrs Cherry Owen

The vitality of this relationship does not arise from any kind of friction or frustration, but from amicable union. When, after a night of heavy

*Douglas Cleverdon, *The Growth of Milk Wood*, Dent, London, 1969, p. 67.

drinking (seventeen pints seems not abnormal, p. 76), her husband returns to their one-room home in Donkey Street much the worse for wear, Mrs Owen not only welcomes him with open arms but also enjoys reminding him the next day of how he threw sago at an aunt's picture and spilled stout and eels all over the floor (p. 31). Captain Cat identifies Mrs Owen by the sound of her cheerful morning step, 'off she trots new as a daisy' (p. 39), but to see this marriage as the only ideal one in Llareggub because the couple are always laughing delightedly together (p. 32) is to mistake the author's purpose. Mr and Mrs Pugh are equally happy together, albeit, as Thomas pointed out in his letter to *Botteghe Oscure*, their marriage is successful for very different reasons (see under *Themes*, p. 42, above).

Other characters

Ocky Milkman, who is more comic in keeping his wife in the cupboard with the empties (p. 43) than in watering down the town's milk with supplies from the river Dewi (see Captain Cat's rather feeble pun, p. 40), says only three words (in his dream, p. 16); otherwise he is merely reported on by the First or Second Voices, who similarly characterise other minor figures in the play. Evans the Death's innocuous dream of childhood (pp. 7–8) declares a sensibility unsuited to his profession as undertaker: he has to press hard 'on the coffin of his breast in case his heart jumps out' (p. 44); Mr and Mrs Floyd, the cocklers, sleep together 'like two old kippers in a box' (p. 16); and the dreaming Attila Rees is so oblivious of his duties that he uses his policeman's helmet as a chamberpot (pp. 16–17). Of the remaining voices that are heard, only those among 'the naughty forfeiting children' (p. 52) are identified by name: Gwennie acts as spokesman for the chorus of girls who hound down Billy, Johnnie Cristo and Dicky with their taunting rhymes (pp. 52–5). An old man (p. 34), a fisherman (p. 47), a child noticing Captain Cat's tears (p. 66), and a drinker in the Sailors Arms (p. 76) have one line each to say; and near the end of the play one woman soothes a child to sleep while a second woman pointedly stresses the meaning of a nursery song, which is about death, by replacing the word 'baby' with 'grandpa':

> When the bough breaks the cradle will fall
> Down will come grandpa, whiskers and all. (p. 75)

Style

> It is impossible to be too clear. I am trying for more clarity now. At first I thought it enough to leave an impression of sound and feeling and let the meaning seep in later, but since I have been giving these

> broadcasts and reading other men's poetry as well as my own, I find it better to have more meaning at first reading.*

The move to greater clarity in his poetry, which Dylan Thomas here partly attributes to his experience in radio broadcasting, was already under way in his prose style by the publication of *Portrait of the Artist as a Young Dog* (1940). Principally, it meant a greater directness of meaning in the choice of words and in the logical relationships between them. What impedes the reader's understanding of Thomas's early stories is the fact that although the grammatical structure of his sentences is normally quite straightforward, the links between individual words in those sentences frequently come from mood, image, and sound rather than from any immediately comprehensible sequence of thought. The following passage, which in places echoes lines from Gerard Manley Hopkins's (1844–89) poem 'That Nature is a Heraclitean Fire', is taken from the story, 'A Prospect of the Sea', published in 1937:

> He walked to the last rail before pitch space; though the earth bowled round quickly, he saw every plough crease and beast's print, man track and waterdrop, comb, crest, and plume mark, dust and death groove and signature and time-cast shade, from icefield to icefield, sea rims to sea centres, all over the apple-shaped ball under the metal rails beyond the living doors.†

What at first sight appears to be a collision between a coherently ordered syntax and a choice of words which seems to have little to do with logic contributes to the surrealistic‡ effect of several of Thomas's early stories, particularly where there is an additional incongruity among the images used. Both the content and the style of the largely autobiographical *Portrait* stories are more down-to-earth than such writing; in them the poet recreates the sensitive ambivalence of adolescent experience without at any time becoming obtrusively individualistic. He was, however, never able to repeat their success in tone or subject. From this point on, prose for Thomas became a work-a-day matter. He is a more versatile prose writer than poet, but at a lower level of achievement which increasingly after 1940 involved him with a public audience as scriptwriter for both film and radio. In sharp contrast to his agonisingly slow process of building a poem – he once admitted to Vernon Watkins that it had taken him three weeks to write the first line

*Quoted in E. W. Tedlock, *Dylan Thomas: The Legend and the Poet*, Heinemann, London, 1960, p. 62.

†Dylan Thomas, *A Prospect of the Sea and other Stories and Prose Writings*, ed. Daniel Jones, Dent, London, 1955, p. 8.

‡Surrealism refers to a movement in twentieth-century literature and art that attempts to exhibit the workings of the subconscious mind, and is characterised by the incongruous arrangement and presentation of subject-matter.

of 'In the White Giant's Thigh' – he wrote comic prose at speed, revising only when whole sections were complete. After the publication in 1952 of his *Collected Poems*, Thomas told Daniel Jones that he had decided to turn his verse away from its intensely personal focus to a more public form of expression; but he never lived to fulfil this aim. What he did do however, was to combine in *Under Milk Wood* his prose gift for humorous observations of life with his poetic gift for evocative language. The writing is far less subtle than the *Portrait* stories, and far less profound than the poetry; but it was not intended to match either. For all its international success, the play was for its author in the main both trivial and trivialising; stylistically, it is more of a *tour de force* than a work dedicated and intrinsic excellence.

Apart from the parody employed in the two sets of verses spoken by the Reverend Eli Jenkins (see the comments on his character, p. 47 above), there are three main kinds of writing in *Under Milk Wood*: the descriptive style of the First and Second Voices, the style of the dialogue, and that of the songs. The first of these is nearest to the style of Thomas's poetry; relying heavily on such devices as imagery and sound, rhythm, assonance and alliteration, the language of the commentaries sometimes risks being too inflated for its subject-matter. In an interview with a journalist during the summer of 1953 Thomas himself wittily characterised it as 'prose with blood pressure'; but he knew very well that words for the ear alone work at different levels of appeal from words for the page or for the stage, and that the linguistic and aural flamboyance of the introductory and descriptive commentaries of the radio play provides both lure and stimulus for its audience.

The fact that repetitively decorative patterns of speech help to attract a listening audience explains one of the principal differences between Dylan Thomas's poetry and the 'poetic' prose of the 'Play for Voices'. In a letter written in 1938 to Henry Treece, the first critic to bring out a full-length study of his work, Thomas described his method of writing poetry as follows:

> I make one image – though 'make' is not the word, I let, perhaps, an image be 'made' emotionally in me and then apply to it what intellectual and critical forces I possess – let it breed another, let that image contradict the first, make of the third image bred out of the other two together, a fourth contradictory image, and let them all, within my imposed formal limits, conflict. Each image holds within it the seeds of its own destruction.*

In contrast, the central images used by the First and Second Voices in *Under Milk Wood* proliferate freely at a very simple level without any

*Quoted in Constantine Fitzgibbon, *Selected Letters of Dylan Thomas*, Dent, London, 1966, p. 191.

kind of dialectical contradiction or opposition. For example, the first paragraph of the play, which contrasts the stillness and silence of the sleeping town with the ceaseless motion of the sea and the night-time activity of lovers, rabbits, and underground moles, evokes the sense of darkness by repeating the word 'black' in four different contexts:

> It is spring, moonless night in the small town, starless and bible-black, the cobblestreets silent and the hunched, courters'-and-rabbits' wood limping invisible down to the sloeblack, slow, black, crowblack, fishingboat-bobbing sea.

Only the first of these says more than one thing at a time (see 'bible-black', Notes and Glossary, p. 19, above); the next three repetitions of the word have much the same meaning, but an additional effect is achieved through the spoken rhythm of the phrase as a whole, which suggests the ebb and flow of the sea. The next two sentences accumulate adjectival terms which suggest dark, or sleep, or silence: 'blind' (twice), 'velvet', 'muffled', 'in mourning', 'widows' weeds', 'lulled', and 'dumbfound'; and seven further repetitions of the word 'black', or near synonyms for it like 'blinded' and 'bandaged', occur in the remainder of the First Voice's introductory description.

This opening paragraph, whose rhythm, alliteration, and assonance are in the main controlled by broad vowel sounds and soft *s*'s, *m*'s, and *f*'s (an exception being the hard *b*'s and *g*'s together with the short *i*'s in 'fishingboat-bobbing') provides a striking contrast with the opening of scene III (p. 41), which describes the activity of the morning in sharp consonants and abrupt vowels; or with the languorous effects in meaning and pronunciation of the images of satiety at the beginning of scene IV (pp. 61–2). Repetitive in nature and primarily descriptive in function, this writing is not designed to be profound; occasionally, however, it reaches beyond its normal limits: at the very end of the play, when night falls again on Llareggub and the wood is awake with lovers, the antithetical images of darkness/death and love/life come near to paradox.

Various kinds of onomatopoeic effects are used to enhance the meaning and mood of the imagery governing the introductory commentaries, and numerous other stylistic devices work towards the particular kind of verbal and aural density achieved in each paragraph. Stemming from Thomas's early interest in surrealism, two of these concern the unusual juxtaposition of words. Unlike surrealism, however, the resultant incongruity is not made to shock or to jar the senses; most often it is merely to joke, but it can demonstrate unforeseen relationships between images or ideas.

At its best, the device of the transferred epithet, a common feature of Thomas's poetry, brings about the condensing of two experiences in a single description. For example, in the second paragraph on page 1, the noun 'aisles' and the adjective 'organplaying' are shifted from their normal context into a new one: 'Young girls lie . . . bridesmaided by glow-worms down the aisles of the organplaying wood.' Because the controlling image has to do with churches, the girls' dreams of love-making in Milk Wood are given the sanctity of wedlock; at the same time, the suggestion that the place of love comes before the place of religion is reinforced by the sexual innuendo in the word 'organplaying'.

A similar but simpler device replaces one or more elements of a common expression with something unexpected. Where the substitution of a new element for an old one occurs in such a way that the old lurks in the mind as an undertone or extension of meaning, there can be an intensification of feeling, as in the ironic echoes of the Second Voice's comment on the re-appearance of the drowned dead and of the ghost of Rosie Probert in Captain Cat's dreams: 'Listen to the night breaking' (see Notes and Glossary, pp. 33–4 above). More frequently, however, Thomas uses this device merely for apt comic effect, as in the description of Mrs Ogmore-Pritchard as 'big-besomed to engage the dust' (p. 29). Sometimes the substitution occurs in one of the elements of a simile which has become a cliché, as with 'quiet as a domino', or 'sharp as sciatica' (see Notes and Glossary, p. 20 and p. 30 above). Occasionally it can descend to a simple play on words which conveys little additional meaning: 'Only *your* eyes are unclosed to see the black and folded town fast, and slow, asleep' (p. 2); and the simplest method of all juxtaposes one word in a list incongruously with the next: 'the undertaker and the fancy woman, drunkard, dressmaker, preacher . . .' (p. 1); 'custard, buckets, henna, rat-traps, shrimp-nets, sugar, stamps, confetti, paraffin, hatchets, whistles.' (p. 41).

Devices which grammatically increase the energy of the descriptions include nouns being transformed into adjectives or verbs, which again compresses meaning so that two things can be said at once; for example, 'the jollyrodgered sea'; 'Mrs Dai Bread Two gypsies up in his mind's slow eye, dressed only in a bangle' (see Notes and Glossary, p. 20 and p. 32 above). In personifying the night as 'royally winding through the Coronation cherry trees' (lightly ironic about the fact that it is usually the poorest streets which are so named), and the winds as 'tumbling by the Sailors Arms' (p. 2), the First Voice creates the sense of everything happening at the very moment in which it is being described by using numerous present participles, no less than ten of which occur within the lower half of page 2 of the text: '. . . hymning in bonnet and brooch . . . coughing like nannygoats, sucking mintoes, fortywinking . . .'.

The dialogue in the play uses a number of techniques similar to those listed above, but it nonetheless presents a contrast of tone, pitch, and language to the descriptive commentaries, and is much more direct and down-to-earth. Rather than an exchange of viewpoints or ideas, what we generally get in *Under Milk Wood* is an interweaving of characters who spend most of their time talking about themselves, whether in their dreams or in their day-dreaming. Where speakers do share a common topic, as in the separate sequence of voices, the rapidity of the contrapuntal exchanges exposes Anglo-Welsh speech patterns even more markedly than in the 'monlogues' spoken by individual characters:

FIRST NEIGHBOUR
Poor Mrs Waldo
SECOND NEIGHBOUR
What she puts up with
FIRST NEIGHBOUR
Never should of married
SECOND NEIGHBOUR
If she didn't had to (p. 9)

This is particularly evident when Captain Cat imitates the gossip of the townswomen:

> Who's having a baby, who blacked whose eye, seen Polly Garter giving her belly an airing, there should be a law, seen Mrs Beynon's new mauve jumper, it's her old grey jumper dyed, who's dead, who's dying, there's a lovely day, oh the cost of soapflakes! (p. 40)

This is not the kind of dialogue traditionally found in plays which attempt to reproduce actual conversation. The idiomatic authenticity which is essential to the vitality of the 'Play for Voices' brought something new to modern drama. Here is Mrs Organ Morgan talking to her husband about Polly Garter (but he is not listening, so she is really talking to herself):

> And when you think of all those babies she's got, then all I can say is she'd better give up bird nesting that's all I can say, it isn't the right kind of hobby at all for a woman that can't say No even to midgets. Remember Bob Spit? He wasn't any bigger than a baby and he gave her two. But they're two nice boys, I will say that, Fred Spit and Arthur. Sometimes I like Fred best and sometimes I like Arthur. Who do you like best, Organ?

ORGAN MORGAN
Oh, Bach without any doubt. Bach every time for me. (pp. 59–60)

Not until the advent of Harold Pinter, whose first play, *The Caretaker*, was produced in 1960, did English stage theatre follow Thomas's lead; and television serials such as 'Coronation Street' could still learn from *Under Milk Wood* about the way language usage defines character and social background.

Although the contrast between the descriptive writing and the ensuing dialogue is most apparent at the openings of scenes I, III and IV, it is frequently noticeable in the speech of a particular character following the introduction by one of the Voices, as in this example:

SECOND VOICE

Gossamer Beynon high-heels out of school . . . . She blazes naked past the Sailors Arms, the only woman on the Dai-Adamed earth. Sinbad Sailors places on her thighs still dewdamp from the first mangrowing cock-crow garden his reverent goat-bearded hands.

GOSSAMER BEYNON

I don't care if he *is* common,

SECOND VOICE

she whispers to her salad-day deep self,

GOSSAMER BEYNON

I want to gobble him up. I don't care if he *does* drop his aitches (p. 56)

Like the narrative commentary, which rarely is concerned simply with a sequence of events (one of the few exceptions being when we are first introduced to the Reverend Eli Jenkins, pp. 22–3), the dialogue has little to do with action. As there is no dramatic conflict, dialogue is not used in order to define a character's motives but to illustrate his disposition. Whether or not it occurs in dreams, dialogue is presented in a manner similar to the 'stream-of-consciousness' writing of James Joyce: an interior monologue which reveals the speaker's eccentric preoccupations.

The songs in the play, on the other hand, are more objective and impersonal. At first hearing, their meaning is immediate and unambiguous; but, like the simple nursery and children's songs on which they are modelled, under the hard and clear emphases of rhyme, rhythm, line length and syllable count they can express a variety of moods, from the evocative yearning of Polly Garter (p. 50) to the vigour of Mr Waldo's song about the 'chimbley-sweep', with its suggestive double-meanings (pp. 76–7); or from the rather tender irony of a woman's voice singing 'Rockabye, grandpa, in the tree top' (p. 75) to the harsh and near savage attack of the girls taunting the boy Dicky:

Put him in the river
Up to his liver
Quick quick Dirty Dick
Beat him on the bum
With a rhubarb stick. (p. 55)

The figurative commentary which immediately follows elaborately conjures up the boy's sexual vulnerability, but it is the rhyming song which creates the realism of the experience.

Part 4

Hints for study

General advice

There are three basic questions to ask about a literary work, as about any work of art: what, why, and how? When we ask 'what?', we are enquiring about form and genre, which concerns *subject*; when we ask 'why?', we are trying to discover what the author wants to say about his chosen subject, or by means of it, which concerns *theme*; when we ask 'how?', we are examining the methods the author uses in order to say what he wants to say, which concerns *style*. The theme of a work emerges through consideration of its style in relation to its subject; and it is the delicate interdependence of these three aspects which defines its uniqueness. While many works may share the same subject-matter (you could easily find, for example, half a dozen poems on the subject of love, or war, or suffering), few share the same attitude to that subject, which means theme; and while some works may use similar devices of style, none uses those same devices for the same theme about the same subject: the only work which exactly matches *Under Milk Wood* in subject (including form and genre), theme, and style is *Under Milk Wood*.

The play is particularly vulnerable to two misinterpretations regarding the inter-relationships of these factors. Much of the divergence of opinion about it stems from mistaken notions about what kind of literature it is and what its aims are – that is why the *Commentary* section in these Notes begins by emphasising the play's distinctiveness as a piece written specifically for the broadcasting medium – but the dependency of Thomas's style in his 'Play for Voices' on sound, word association, imagery, and allusion brings the additional danger that a critic may be tempted to excessive weighting in his reading of its meaning. For example, the opening statement, 'To begin at the beginning', consciously echoes a biblical text, but to attribute to it the Word of the Artist Creator speaking to the faith of a people's imagination would be a gross inflation of the intended meaning. As in all art forms, the interpretation of any part of the play has to be governed by an interpretation of the whole; and in this case the allusion is limited by its links in the rest of the play with the theme of innocence, which most of the time is presented in the tone of light parody.

This kind of misreading can lead to more serious errors of judgment, as is everywhere demonstrated in David Holbrook's attacks on the play in his book, *Llareggub Revisited* (Bowes & Bowes, London, 1962). Mr Holbrook persists in making totally inappropriate comparisons of Thomas's play with Joyce's *Ulysses* (1922): he reads far too much into an allusion, then castigates Thomas for not sustaining the terms of that misreading. This critic fails to see from the start that despite superficial resemblances (the treatment of twenty-four hours in the life of a community, the use of some of Joyce's techniques, verbal echoes and parallel incidents), *Under Milk Wood* is a completely different work from *Ulysses* in subject, form and genre, and in theme and style.

An even more serious kind of error can occur, however, if a reference is taken out of context and used as evidence for something the critic himself wishes to establish. In his second book on Dylan Thomas, *The Code of Night* (Athlone Press, London, 1972), seeking evidence for what he calls Thomas's 'schizoid condition', Mr Holbrook produces flagrant misreadings of several points of comic detail in the play. With reference to Dancing Williams's comment 'I lost my step in Nantucket' (p. 3), he says: 'He lost his (dancing) step by losing his existential foothold, as Thomas did in America'; and about Nogood Boyo's never having caught anything when out fishing except a Mrs Samuels, who had 'been in the water a week' (p. 43), Mr Holbrook remonstrates: 'Is a corpse which has been in the water a week still a "Mrs Samuels"? This is at root a disturbing existential question.' The only sane response to such absurd claims is to read them as some kind of comic skit on the comedy of the play; but to do so means misinterpreting the subject, theme, and style of Mr Holbrook's criticism as thoroughly as he has unwittingly misinterpreted all these elements in Dylan Thomas's radio play.

Employing one of Thomas's favourite tricks of word substitution, Daniel Jones's chapter heading, 'Overmilk'd Wood'* fittingly characterises such excessive and wayward readings of the play. The lessons to be learned, however, are very clear: the fact that a critic's viewpoint gets into print doesn't mean that you should let it go unchallenged; and to challenge someone else's ideas means that you must have a coherent reading of your own from which to work. The first essential is to read the play for yourself, without any preconception or prejudice and without any kind of critical aid. However fragmentary your initial understanding may be, this first reading provides a unique encounter with the work which can give something of the sense of wonder described in Keats's (1795–1821) famous sonnet, 'On First Looking into Chapman's Homer'. Later readings should bring you to the point where you can not only easily identify any part of the play but also define its function with relation to the subject, themes, and style of the work as a whole. Only when you have reached this stage are you best able to benefit from whatever relevant criticism you can find, which may bring about a

*Daniel Jones, *My Friend Dylan Thomas*, Dent, London, 1977, pp. 82–94.

modification or extension of your own views. But you must never read critical opinion passively, nor merely learn it off by rote. The validity of any viewpoint must always be assessed by examining it in context, by testing it against the mood, tone, and meaning of the play itself.

All these exercises have the one purpose of bringing you closer to *Under Milk Wood*: the play doesn't alter, but you do, as your understanding grows. Critical awareness cannot, however, be achieved without vigilant enquiry into what your responses are to the work and to other people's commentaries on it. After your first or second reading of the play you should begin to note down your interpretation of its different aspects: for one thing, if you don't take notes you are likely to forget much of what you were thinking as you were reading; for another, it is very useful practice for examinations to force yourself to give cogent expression to your ideas; lastly, putting a thought down in writing is the crucial test of its coherence and relevance. You may find it helpful to keep a separate section of your notes for questions that occur to you about the play or that come out of your discussions with friends or from your reading of criticism about it. A good question should reveal new facets about the work you are studying, acting like a mine-shaft of enquiry into its composition and texture.

Topics and essay questions

In the following list of twenty topics, the first four are mainly concerned with 'character', the next four with 'theme', the next six with 'style', and the last six with 'form and genre':

(1) List as many contrasts in character as you can find in the play, such as Polly Garter/Gossamer Beynon, Mr and Mrs Cherry Owen/Mr and Mrs Pugh, Jack Black/Mr Waldo, Mary Ann Sailors/Lord Cut-Glass, giving a brief analysis of each.

(2) Find a quotation for each of the main characters which illustrates a notable action or attitude; for example, Butcher Beynon's teasing of his wife may be remembered by 'owlmeat, dogs' eyes, manchop' (p. 18); the realism of Lily Smalls's view of herself can be shown by any of the lines from her dialogue with herself (p. 25); the poignancy of Polly Garter's memories is revealed by the refrain of her song (p. 50); and the allure of Mrs Dai Bread Two is epitomised in the phrase 'gypsied to kill' (p. 28).

(3) Note how each character is defined by comically exaggerated emphasis on his trade, hobby or personal preoccupation, which in turn is frequently further illustrated by the name he is given. What, for example, is appropriate about the names Willy Nilly, Organ Morgan and Jack Black, and what action best characterises each?

(4) Analyse the functions of Captain Cat and the Reverend Eli Jenkins as members of the community and as observers of it.

(5) Select what you consider to be the most serious and the most comic incidents and/or statements in the play and comment where appropriate on their relevance to its themes. In Polly Garter's complaint, 'Nothing grows in our garden, only washing. And babies' (p. 29), the comic juxtaposition emphasises the theme of innocence; similarly, the picture of Lord Cut-Glass in his crazy kitchen speaks of the psychological threat presented by the consciousness of Time (pp. 60–1). Occasionally, the comedy falls away completely for a moment or two, as in Rosie Probert's 'I am going into the darkness of the darkness for ever. I have forgotten that I was ever born' (p. 66).

(6) Establish links between different characters which point to any of the play's themes. What, for example, is the author saying about innocence and experience through Polly Garter and Rosie Probert, or Bessie Bighead and Mary Ann Sailors?

(7) Examine what contribution to the play's themes is made by the descriptive commentary of the First and Second Voices. The First Voice's praise of Bessie Bighead (p. 70), for example, very specifically underlines Thomas's concept of Llareggub as an Arcadia; while the description of Captain Cat climbing into his bunk, where 'Through the voyages of his tears he sails to see the dead' (p. 77), emphasises the need to defeat Time by creating an awareness of the past in the present.

(8) List the main references in the play to Time, Loss and Death.

(9) In what ways is the listener made aware of the presence of the sea? Your notes here should include not only the alliterative and onomatopoeic devices used for example by the First Voice in the introduction, but also the effects of later passages, such as the Second Voice's description of the harbour (pp. 46–7), as well as the number of times the setting is evoked by less detailed references, such as the picture of babies and old men being wheeled on to 'the sunlit cockled cobbles' (p. 34).

(10) List the different kinds of poetic devices used and give a brief illustration of each.

(11) Examine the different kinds of verse used in the play, commenting on both style and purpose. The exchange between Captain Cat and Rosie Probert, for example, is in the form of rhyming questions and answers (pp. 64–5), very repetitive in form and using many nouns and very few verbs. The result is clarity and strength of statement, speed and lightness of expression, conveying the delight of their relationship; this provides a striking contrast to the image of dissolution with which the dead Rosie ends the conversation.

(12) List the images of innocence, giving a brief interpretation of the ways in which they are linked in meaning. Where else in the play, for example, is imagery suggesting Paradise to be found, apart from the specific reference to the Garden of Eden (p. 20)?

(13) Choose any one passage of about a page in length, and examine what appeals are made to the eye and ear of the listener; where appropriate, try to determine which images and sounds control and unify the description, as in the opening evocation of darkness and sleep (pp. 1–3), or in the sharp and harsh sounds of the Second Voice's picture of the prussic plots of Mr Pugh (pp. 62–3).

(14) Illustrate some of the ways in which language usage helps to define character and social background. See Part 3, p. 40 above, for comments on Anglo-Welsh speech patterns in the play. You should also try to determine how a particular character's personality and disposition are conveyed by the words he uses. What, for example, is the difference in the way each of Dai Bread's two wives introduces herself (p. 28)?

(15) All the stage directions in *Under Milk Wood* have to do with sound effects. Select a number of these from different parts of the play and comment on the contribution each makes to the listener's response at the appropriate juncture. For instance, after the comic echo of the last words in James Joyce's *Ulysses* represented by Myfanwy Price's gasping avowal 'Yes, Mog, yes, Mog, yes, yes, yes' (p. 7), the noise of money-tills and chapel bells is heard, as announced by Mog himself, in justly ironic celebration of the draper's preoccupation with trade having invaded his proposal of marriage.

(16) What modifications of the play's structure would you suggest for a stage or television performance? See Part 3, pp. 35–6 above, for comments on ways to lessen some of the problems caused by such adaptations of the 'Play for Voices'.

(17) Note where the commentary of either of the two Voices gives the listener a camera's view of the scene, and try to establish what particular techniques are being employed; as for example in the shifts made in the opening description from a cinematographic 'panning' of the whole setting to the separate and intimate 'close-ups' of the boats at anchor, of the chapel, and of the 'blinded bedrooms' (pp. 1–3).

(18) Contrast is one of basic comic methods used in the play. Select examples of contrast in character and in scene, and comment on the effect of each. Immediately after the picture of Mr Waldo's promiscuity (pp. 8–13), we are introduced to the inhibiting fastidiousness of Mrs Ogmore-Pritchard, followed by Gossamer Beynon's sensual dreams. Juxtaposing the one against the other makes us aware of the variety of characters living in Llareggub, but

at the same time the comic exaggeration forces us to recognise that each portrait is not without its truth to human nature. A good example of contrast in setting is provided at the opening of scene II when the First Voice's evocative prose is followed by the clichés of the Voice of a Guide-Book (pp. 21–2). Here Thomas's purpose is to mock the conventional kind of description found in travel brochures while stressing the distinctiveness of his own style.

(19) List the different kinds of comic effect achieved in the play, such as comedy of language, of behaviour, of situation, or of action, giving striking examples of each.

(20) In order to deflate the seriousness which emerges at a number of points in the play, Thomas immediately juxtaposes comic detail. Note where this occurs and at what stage in the development of any of the themes. Against Captain Cat's yearning cry 'Come back, come back', for example, we hear the child's observation 'He's crying all over his nose' (p. 66); and after the powerful image given to the Second Voice, 'Listen to the night breaking' (p. 78: see Notes and Glossary for comments on this line), Organ Morgan mistakes the drunken Cherry Owen for his favourite composer, Bach, lying on a tombstone. These two incidents involving Captain Cat express more intensely than anywhere else in the play the theme of recognition of loss; for a brief moment the characters are without the disguise of dreams or of linguistic flamboyance, and in each case it is the loss of love which elicits the stark realism of statement or image. For such notes to be sounded more frequently in *Under Milk Wood* would have meant completely changing the tone and mood of the play; that they are there at all is a tribute to the range of effects the author is able to achieve in what after all was never intended to be anything other than a spirited if novel form of comic drama.

Taking notes on these topics, thinking about the different aspects of the play which are involved, and giving your own commentary and analysis will prepare you for answering more comprehensive essay questions. The following list contains five questions on character, ten on theme, five on style, and five on form and genre:

(1) 'The "community" of *Under Milk Wood* is a group of very diverse entertainers who don't live together at all.' Do you agree?

(2) 'There is no realism of character portrayal in Thomas's play: it is all caricature and dreams, with no truth to human nature.' Discuss.

(3) Examine the variety of roles played by different women characters in *Under Milk Wood*, distinguishing how far each contributes towards the author's themes.

(4) To what extent do you agree with Thomas's own comments on the

characters in the play: 'all, by their own rights, are ordinary and good; and the 1st Voice, and the poet preacher, never judge nor condemn . . .'?

(5) Compare and contrast the attitudes of the various married couples and assess the main function of each in relation to the play's comedy and/or meaning.

(6) 'The world of *Under Milk Wood* is mere fairy tale or fantasy; it carries no reference to a moral order outside its own existence, presents no conflict between right and wrong, and therefore can teach us nothing.' Discuss the relevance of this view and state in what ways the play may be seen to be both valuable and enjoyable.

(7) Defend the play against the attack that it presents love from a viewpoint which is merely cynical and adolescent.

(8) 'For all its verve and comedy, life in Llareggub is never far from the awareness of death.' Discuss the appropriateness of this comment to the play's action and themes.

(9) 'Thomas's picture of Welsh life in *Under Milk Wood* is built upon a basic opposition between the Puritan and the sensualist.' Do you agree?

(10) In what ways is the recurring fear of Time assuaged in the play?

(11) 'Without overstressing anything, Thomas has hinted at how it is all idealised – because it is a dream, because it is Eden, because it is childhood; and also without making it too unreal.' How far would you agree with this view?

(12) Examine how different kinds of comedy, including parody, protect the play from sentimentality of attitude and meaning.

(13) Resolve the apparent contradictions between these quotations from the play: 'Oh, isn't life a terrible thing, thank God?' (Polly Garter, p. 29); 'There's a nasty lot live here when you come to think' (Fourth Woman, p. 42); 'We are not wholly bad or good/Who live our lives under Milk Wood' (Reverend Eli Jenkins, p. 73).

(14) Examine different examples of the linking together of the themes concerning Time, Loss and Death, and consider whether they at any time threaten to dislodge the play's evocation of innocence.

(15) What for you is the most realistic aspect of the play? Discuss whether or not, and for what reasons, this is also the most comic or serious element in it.

(16) 'Prose with blood pressure.' How relevant do you consider Thomas's own comment is about his style in *Under Milk Wood*?

(17) Contrast the style of the two Voices with that of the dialogue in the play and point out the purpose of each.

(18) Choose a representative section of any one scene in the play and make a detailed analysis of its stylistic effects with relation both to mood and to meaning.

(19) 'Above all, it is variety of style that keeps the play alive: it changes the pace of its production, and is the basis of its entertainment.' Discuss.

(20) 'All the characters speak alike; they are as indistinguishable in language as are the voices of the drowned sailors, the four neighbours, the four women, and those of the children, all of which act as a kind of chorus commentary on the play.' Do you agree?

(21) What features of this play mark it out as being especially written for radio?

(22) '*Under Milk Wood* is not dramatic in any sense of the word; it is episodic.' How far do you agree with this comment, and in what ways do you consider that the play is structured?

(23) Distinguish between the several different kinds of commentary in the play, indicating differences of viewpoint, attitude and style, as for instance between the First Voice and Captain Cat.

(24) Discuss the function of each of the four separate sequences of voices and comment on the effect of the mixture of their commentary with scraps of dialogue.

(25) 'The flaw is in the part of the narrator. Even in its original form, the play's use of this device was unsatisfying; and on the stage, where personality is less easily suppressed, it stands out with irrelevant prominence' (from a review of a stage production of *Under Milk Wood* in *The Times*). Discuss the different needs of different kinds of production of the play, for the ear or the eye, and assess the value of the narrator (that is, of the two Voices) in each.

Planning and writing an essay

Your first task is to make sure you understand all the implications of the question set. Ask yourself what its purpose is, where its emphases lie, what it is trying to uncover about the play, and how far you are prepared to agree with its viewpoint. If you choose a question just because of a single factor in it which appeals to you, you are likely to produce a repetitive and only partial answer, so test your knowledge by jotting down as many different points as you can. Arranged under headings, this list of ideas then becomes the basis for your essay plan. Each section of the essay should be organised under a main topic or broad generalisation which covers a separate area of the question asked. Of course, in literature one thing is never completely divorced from another – for example, writing about the character of Captain Cat inevitably involves consideration of the play's theme and form – but the particular topic of each section should govern what aspects you list under it, such as the analysis of supporting evidence for its point of view, or the assessment of ideas which may challenge it. The order in which you present these details depends exactly upon what you want to emphasise, but make sure there is a logical relation between them. Additional ideas, which will almost certainly occur to you as you write, can then be coherently fitted into your argument.

When you begin writing, don't waste time with irrelevant introductory material: your very first words should show the examiner that you understand why he asked the question, and that you are getting down straight away to answering it. Don't include anything that the question doesn't refer to: there's no point in commenting on the cinematographic techniques employed, no matter how much you know about them, if the question has to do with the different kinds of married love presented in the play.

When you bring in quotations from the text, make sure they are both apt and as brief as need be. First introduce the illustration you want to use, then give the quotation (indenting from the margin if it has to be more than two or three lines long), then analyse its relevance to the argument you are developing. If you quote from a critic or paraphrase his ideas in an essay written at home, you are obliged to include a note saying where the information comes from; but this sort of detail is unnecessary in an examination unless you want to take exception to or show specific agreement with a particular viewpoint.

Above all, don't merely tell the story or say just what the play says. Your job is to interpret what happens or what is described in the play in relation to what you are being asked. For instance, if you are asked about the function of the Second Voice, don't merely tell your reader what the Second Voice tells the listener; your answer here should be concerned with such matters as the variety of approach achieved by alternating the two Voices, what proportion of the commentary is given to description of setting and what to the introduction of the characters, including the different styles employed, and whether you consider the Second Voice at any point obtrusive. At the end of the essay it may be more appropriate to indicate your awareness of other possible fields of enquiry rather than to summarise what you have already said; or, if the essay's structure is complete in itself, no formal conclusion may be necessary.

Finally, a word about your own style. Where possible use the present tense throughout in referring to what the author does with his play and what happens in it. Don't, for example, say: 'Thomas was careful to ensure that the Reverend Eli Jenkins was not openly mocked by any of the other characters'; it is much more straightforward to say: 'Thomas ensures that the Reverend Eli Jenkins is not openly mocked . . .'; don't say: 'When Mr Waldo was dreaming about his childhood, the exchange of dialogue became very fragmented', but: 'When Mr Waldo dreams about . . . dialogue becomes . . . .' Avoid using elaborate language in a mistaken effort to impress your examiner. Clarity and directness in your writing will help to provide coherence and continuity for your thought; but at the same time, enthusiasm for the subject coupled with intellectual honesty about your reactions to the question you are answering can bring an individual quality to your style which examiners readily recognise and reward.

All these principles about planning and writing an essay apply to work you do at home as well as to examinations; you will find it useful, however, to practise answering questions under set time limits and without your text to hand. If you are ever unfortunate enough to run out of time in an examination, remember it is far better to finish two questions partially in note form than to write a full essay on one and leave the other unanswered.

Specimen essay plans

First of all, here is a very simple plan for a straightforward answer to question (3) in the list above: 'Examine the variety of roles played by different women characters in *Under Milk Wood*, distinguishing how far each contributes towards the author's themes.' The sections of the plan provide for different angles of investigation, but you must remember that you have to make a selection from the characters in the play for your examples; you can't bring them all in.

(*a*) *Differences in status*
Married women's attitudes to their husbands
Single women's attitudes to men
Women as commentators
(*b*) *Functions of contrast*
Mrs Pugh and Mrs Cherry Owen
Rosie Probert and Gossamer Beynon
Polly Garter and Bessie Bighead
(*c*) *Attitudes of men towards women*
Games of war: the forfeiting children (scene III)
Frustration: in adolescence (Nogood Boyo); in adulthood (Sinbad)
Fantasy: Mog Edwards
Marriage: Organ Morgan, Mr Pugh, Cherry Owen
Promiscuity: Waldo
Puritanism: Jack Black
Loss: Captain Cat
(*d*) *Women and themes*
No condemnation of marriage, nor of love outside marriage
Mary Ann Sailors and the theme of Innocence
Rosie Probert and the themes of Loss and Death

The next plan is for a more difficult question, number (8) in the list, which concentrates much more on meaning and on mood than on character: '"For all its verve and comedy, life in Llareggub is never far from the awareness of death." Discuss the appropriateness of this comment to the play's action and themes.'

(*a*) *Structure of the play*
Cyclical movement from darkness of opening to darkness at end
Morning setting of scene II relatively free of references to Death
Until Polly Garter's song (p. 50), scene III characterised by Mary Ann Sailors's happy ignorance of Time, and by the glee-party singing in the graveyard (p. 45 and p. 48)
Death increasingly invoked through latter part of scene III to end of scene IV
(*b*) *Identification with death in scene I*
Sleep as Death (as well as dream)
The drowned dead: white bone and skull talking (p. 3)
Emphasis on Time: in commentary, in Captain Cat's dreams, in comic echo of Marvell's poem (p. 7), in Lord Cut-Glass's closing words: 'Tick tock tick tock . . .'
(*c*) *Intensification of references to death*
Refrain of Polly Garter's song echoes through the rest of play (pp. 50, 52, 61, 79)
Scene III ends with comic expression of fear (Lord Cut-Glass's kitchen) and poignant expression of loss (Polly Garter)
Dialogues between Captain Cat and Rosie Probert (pp. 63–6, 77–8)
Images of Loss and Death (pp. 66, 70, 71, 78)
Sleep identified with Death in transposed nursery rhyme (p. 75)
(*d*) *Escape from death*
The attempt to defeat Time by reliving the past in the present (Captain Cat's and Mr Waldo's dreams)
Antithesis of Death/night and Life/love at end of play which points to a profound paradox: the 'live dusk of this place of love'
Two elements at work throughout the play: comic juxtaposition deflates its serious tone; sexuality and love seen as forces which oppose that of Death (give examples of each). Conclude with illustration of both elements combined (p. 75: old unwinking men watching for death, and unmarried girls decking themselves for the Dance of the World).

You can refer to Part 3 and to the brief examples given of answers to the topics listed in order to help you to expand the main points of each of these two essay plans. The third plan, below, for an answer to question (19) in the list, is followed by a short essay based upon it.

Specimen plan and essay

'Above all, it is variety of style that keeps the play alive: it changes the pace of its production, and is the basis of its entertainment.' Discuss.

PLAN:

(*a*) *Versatility of style*
Descriptive commentary
Dialogue
Songs
(*b*) *Functions of different styles*
The Voices: as 'montage' and as narrative
Dialogue: as character and as commentary
Songs: distinctions in mood and meaning
Best examples of each style combine effects of each aspect
(*c*) *Changes in style*
Contrasts:
  between commentary and dialogue
  between images used
  between serious and comic
  between speed of delivery and intonation
(*d*) *Language for radio drama*
New medium needs new methods: in defence of the narrators
Minimal use of non-verbal sound effects
Language usage governed by appeal to ear as much as to mind
Necessity for emphasis and variety
Radio as the ideal medium for Dylan Thomas

ESSAY:

Of all Dylan Thomas's prose pieces, including stories, radio talks and film scripts, *Under Milk Wood* is stylistically the most versatile, a fact which explains why it is also the most successful. In the main, there are three kinds of writing employed: the descriptive style of the First and Second Voices as commentators, the style of the dialogue, and that of the songs in the play. Distinctions between these are directly related to their different functions.

Because the commentators' primary role is to introduce the setting to the listener, their language is vividly evocative, drawing heavily upon effects of imagery, sound patterns, rhythm, word association, assonance and alliteration. In addition, the First Voice's incantatory repetition of 'Look . . . Listen' at the opening of the play wilfully lures the radio audience into a secret and privileged position of intimacy with the sleeping town and the dreams of its eccentric inhabitants. Perhaps too inflated and overich were it intended for reading and not for listening, this style is generally characterised by its density of poetic devices and by its dependency upon governing images, such as those of dark and sleep at the very beginning, and those of satiety in the description of the 'sunny slow lulling afternoon' at the opening of scene IV.

In contrast, the dialogue in the play is freshly idiomatic and straightforward; furthermore, whereas the comedy of the descriptive writing largely comes out of word play of one kind or another, that of the dialogue often relates directly to a character's attitudes and background. But what we hear is more often a person in conversation with himself than with others, much of the dialogue being a sort of interior monologue which reveals a particular, frequently comic, facet of personality.

The style of the songs is markedly different from that of the two Voices; and while some similarities in vigour and directness can be discovered between the language of the dialogue and that of the songs, the latter are distinguished by the formal clarity and objectivity which result from simple patterns of rhyme, rhythm and line length. Further distinctions within each of these main categories provide for yet more detailed differences in function and appeal.

The two Voices not only create what may be called a 'montage' of cumulative sounds and images which usually help to establish the play's major themes (see, for example, pp. 1–3, 60–1, 63, and 71, where each of the commentaries has to do with Time and memories or dreams); they are also used to present comic catalogues of persons or things (see p. 1 and p. 19), as well as occasionally to give pieces of relatively straightforward narrative. What the commentator describes in such scenes as our first introduction to the Reverend Eli Jenkins (pp. 22–3), or to Mr and Mrs Cherry Owen (pp. 30–1), or to the details of Mr Pugh's secretive plans (p. 57), concerns action which illuminates character. On the other hand, the distinction between the language of the two Voices and that of the dialogue is not always as plain as has been claimed. In several places Thomas endows his characters with a poetic flow of words very similar to the style of the descriptive commentaries, as for example when Organ Morgan in his dreams describes, among other instances of 'perturbation and music in Coronation Street', ladies from 'the Women's Welfare hoofing, bloomered, in the moon' (p. 15); or when Mary Ann Sailors dreams of her Eden-like childhood (p. 20); or when Mrs Cherry Owen tells her husband of his return home, 'drunk as a deacon with a big wet bucket and a fish-frail full of stout . . . and then over the bucket you went, sprawling and bawling, and the floor was all flagons and eels.' (p. 31). It is precisely because such eloquence is based upon the linguistic vitality of Anglo-Welsh speech that the language used to identify character has common ground with the more extreme usage of the commentaries and gives that style a recognisable source.

There are ten different kinds of rhyming song in *Under Milk Wood* (see pp. 8, 23–4, 25, 47, 50, 52–5, 64–5, 73, 75, 76–7), and it would take an essay on its own to analyse them in any detail. While they vary widely in tone and mood, one thing they have in common is their unabashed forthrightness of statement and feeling. For all the poignant appeal of Polly Garter's song or of the exchange between Captain Cat and Rosie Probert, and despite the clever parody in Eli Jenkins's verses or the attractive energy in Mr Waldo's song, it is arguable that the most successful sequence is that of the children's voices (pp. 52–5), because it combines the best features of all the songs: hard clarity of meaning, sharpness of outline, and stark realism of character, together with a rapidity of exchange which is particularly enhanced by Daniel Jones's music at this point. Similarly, perhaps the best examples of the very different art of the commentators occur where the verbal flamboyance is given coherence by the description of an actual sequence of events:

> And the shrill girls giggle and master around him and squeal as they clutch and thrash, and he blubbers away downhill with his patched pants falling, and his tear-splashed blush burns all the way as the triumphant bird-like sisters scream with buttons in their claws and the bully brothers hoot after him his little nickname and his mother's shame and his father's wickedness with the loose wild barefoot women of the hovels of the hills. (p. 55)

The pace of the production of the play is largely dependent upon changes from one kind of style to another, one of the most striking of which occurs at the beginning after the First Voice's long introduction, persuasive and inveigling in tone and elaborate in language, when we hear the sharp and increasingly rapid snippets of statements and questions from the drowned sailors in Captain Cat's dreams. (It is worth remembering, too, that the variety within the commentators' approach can be supplemented by alternating between a male and a female voice in appropriate places.) In this sequence, as in all the other sequences of voices, meaning is conveyed as much by intonation as by grammatical syntax, so that just two words can be very evocative: the Fifth Drowned's 'Rock-a-bye baby?' depends for its effect upon its context, but at the same time, like several of the other questions asked by his companions, it has a link with something that happens later in the play; here it is the nursery rhyme about death (p. 75).

The contrast between the serious and the comic which occurs at several points in the play is sometimes carried in the images which are employed, as in the shift in tone from the reiterated relationship between seafaring and sexuality implied in the lighthearted dialogue between Captain Cat and Rosie Probert to the metaphysical image with which she describes her dissolution (pp. 63–6). More frequently such contrasts are brought about by the juxtaposition of entirely different styles, as when the First Voice's gently ironic 'The dead come out in their Sunday best' is immediately followed by the dense image, 'Listen to the night breaking.' (p. 78). No single passage in the play contains examples of all these kinds of contrast in style, but there is a particularly good concentration of commentary and dialogue together with narrative and imagery at the end of scene III (pp. 58–60).

It is equally pointless to attack the structure of *Under Milk Wood* for not being dramatic as to criticise it adversely for not conforming to specific stylistic expectations of the theatre. It is not a novel, nor a stage play; both its form and its style are dictated by its medium, which is sound. Adverse criticism of the narrators' role stems from mistaken attempts to stage the radio play unchanged from its broadcasting format because the listener has to rely on words alone to create the scene, it is essential that several different kinds of language are employed for different functions. The various areas of interest visually provided for in the theatre have to be replaced in broadcasting by numerous and frequent changes of voice, pace, and style. Since Thomas makes relatively little use of non-verbal sound effects in his play, the necessity for such variety is all the more apparent and quite justifies the remarkable range he employs between the descriptive extravagance and curt nursery rhyme. Throughout, the listener is being seduced by sound as much as by meaning. And because from his early childhood the sound of words was at least as important to Dylan Thomas as the things they referred to, radio was his natural medium. But there is another way of explaining the energy and variety of style in the 'Play for Voices'. There is a sense in which the verbal prodigality mirrors the prodigality of nature in the play, as manifested in the sexual awareness of all the characters and their need for love. So style becomes the organic embodiment of theme.

Part 5

Suggestions for further reading

The text

The text used in these Notes is the Everyman paperback:

DYLAN THOMAS: *Under Milk Wood: A Play for Voices*, Prefaces (1954 and 1974) by Daniel Jones, Dent, London, 1977.

Other versions and printings of the play are referred to in 'A note on the text' at the end of Part 1.

Other works by Dylan Thomas, including selections of verse and/or prose

18 Poems, Favil Press, London, 1934.

Twenty-five Poems, Dent, London, 1936.

The Map of Love, Dent, London, 1939 (Stories and poems).

The World I Breathe, New Directions, Norfolk, Conn., 1939 (Limited edition).

Portrait of the Artist as a Young Dog, Dent, London, 1940 (Stories).

New Poems, New Directions, Norfolk, Conn., 1943.

Deaths and Entrances, Dent, London, 1946 (Poems).

Selected Writings, New Directions, New York, 1946 (Stories and poems).

Collected Poems 1934–52, Dent, London, 1952.

In Country Sleep and Other Poems, New Directions, New York, 1952.

Quite Early One Morning, ed. A. N. Davies, Dent, London, 1954 (Radio scripts and readings). An edition published in the same year by New Directions, New York, prints some additional material together with revised versions of several of the radio talks.

A Prospect of the Sea, ed. Daniel Jones, Dent, London, 1955 (A selection of early stories, including the seven published in *The Map of Love*, Dent, London, 1939, with four other prose pieces).

Adventures in the Skin Trade and Other Stories, Putnam, London, 1955.

The Beach of Falésa, Stein & Day, New York, 1963 (Film script).

The Doctor and the Devils, Time Life Books, New York, 1964 (Film script).

Twenty Years A-Growing, Dent, London, 1964 (Film script).

Rebecca's Daughters and *Me and My Bike*, Triton, London, 1968 (Film scripts).

Early Prose Writings, ed. Walford Davies, Dent, London, 1971.

The Poems, ed. Daniel Jones, Dent, London, 1971 (Includes more than a hundred poems additional to the eighty-nine published in *Collected Poems*, Dent, London, 1952).

The Death of the King's Canary, Hutchinson, London, 1976 (Satirical novel written in 1940; co-author, John Davenport).

Reading Dylan Thomas's poetry

A newcomer to the poetry should begin with selections that are fairly readily understandable, such as 'And death shall have no dominion', 'The force that through the green fuse drives the flower', 'Paper and sticks', 'The hunchback in the park', 'Poem in October', 'Fern Hill', 'In my craft or sullen art', and 'Do not go gentle into that good night'. The work of R. S. Thomas, an Anglo-Welsh poet who is an exact contemporary of Dylan Thomas, provides a notable contrast to the latter's poetic style, and in particular to the representation of Welsh village life given in *Under Milk Wood*. See, for example, R. S. Thomas's narrative poem, 'The Minister', in his early selected volume *Song at the Year's Turning*, Hart-Davis, London, 1955.

Letters and biographies

Dylan Thomas: Letters to Vernon Watkins, ed. Vernon Watkins, Dent, London, 1957.

Selected Letters of Dylan Thomas, ed. Constantine Fitzgibbon, Dent, London, 1966.

Twelve More Letters, Daedalus Press, Norfolk, Conn., 1969.

The Life of Dylan Thomas, by Constantine Fitzgibbon, Dent, London, 1965.

Dylan Thomas, by Paul Ferris, Hodder & Stoughton, London, 1977 (Also available in a Penguin Books edition).

Selected criticism

ACKERMAN, J.: *Dylan Thomas: His Life and Work*, Oxford University Press, London, 1964. See the chapter 'The Artist in Comedy', pp. 162–84.

ADAMS, S. (ED.): *Poetry Wales*, Autumn 1973, vol. 9, no. 2, Christopher Davies, Carmarthenshire, 1973. A special Dylan Thomas issue; see the essays by P. E. Lewis, R. Mathias and D. Cleverdon, pp. 27–38, 51–74, and 85–92.

CLEVERDON, D.: *The Growth of Milk Wood*, Dent, London, 1969. An interesting account of the history of the play by its first BBC producer.

COX, C. B. (ED.): *Dylan Thomas: A Collection of Critical Essays*, Prentice Hall, Englewood Cliffs, New Jersey, 1957. See the essays by W. Epsom, R. Williams, and A. Pratt, pp. 84–8, 89–98, and 117–30.

DAVIES, W. (ED.): *Dylan Thomas: New Critical Essays*, Dent, London, 1972. See L. Lerner, 'Sex in Arcadia: *Under Milk Wood*', pp. 262–89.

DAVIES, W.: *Dylan Thomas* (Writers of Wales series), University of Wales Press, Aberystwyth, 1972. A very good introduction to the poet's work, with pertinent references to the radio play.

FRASER, G. S.: *Dylan Thomas*, Longman, London, 1957, revised 1964, 1972. A succinct and perceptive introduction to the poetry.

HOLBROOK, D.: *Llareggub Revisited: Dylan Thomas and the State of Modern Poetry*, Bowes & Bowes, London, 1962; *The Code of Night*, Athlone Press, London, 1972. Both books are given as extreme examples of adverse criticism of the author and of his play.

JONES, T. H.: *Dylan Thomas* (Writers and Critics series), Oliver & Boyd, Edinburgh, 1963. Another good general introduction, containing numerous references to *Under Milk Wood*.

STANFORD, D.: *Dylan Thomas*, Spearman, London, 1954. An early general study which contains some sensible comments on the play.

The author of these notes

COLIN MEIR is Reader in English Literature at Ulster Polytechnic. He is a graduate of Trinity College, Dublin, and of the University of Essex. After teaching at a Manchester grammar school, he became Lecturer in English, then Assistant Professor at McGill University, Montreal, where he gained a Quebec Scholar award during 1965–7. He has taught at St Paul's College, Rugby, at the Polytechnic of Wales, and in the Extramural Departments of Birmingham University and of Queen's University, Belfast. He is the author of *The Ballads and Songs of W. B. Yeats* (1974), and has recently published essays on the poetry of R. S. Thomas, on the stories of William Carleton, and on the poetry and plays of W. B. Yeats.